S0-BFB-239

DISCARD

Seeking Joy

The Real Truth About Work/Life Balance

Women Corporate Executives Speak Out

Get to What's Real. Figure Out the Truth. Plan Joy. Experience Joy.

Seeking Joy

The Real Truth About Work/Life Balance

Women Corporate Executives Speak Out

Rhonda Harper

Rhonda Harper

Published by Global Book Publishing, Charleston, SC, USA.
First Printing, November 2003
2nd Edition September 2004 – includes RTM&J Life/Balance Survey 2004

LIBRARY OF CONGRESS CATALOGING-IN-PUBLICATION DATA

Harper, Rhonda 1961-

Seeking joy: the real truth about work / life balance / by Rhonda Harper

Library of Congress Control Number: 2003098282

ISBN: 1-59457-128-7

Printed in the United States of America.

Editors: This book was conceived, researched, written, and published in eight days. Part of achieving balance is letting go of the idea of perfection.

To order more books:
Additional copies of this book may be purchased from www.rtmj.com as well as book retailers. Bulk orders can be placed by emailing seekingjoy@rtmj.com. Rhonda Harper is available to speak at your event. Contact her at seekingjoy@rtmj.com at RTM&J® Inc.

For Jayne and Jim.

Contents

Preface

Like many people, I've often imagined writing a book. In my case, however, I thought it would be a business book focused on brand management and marketing or a collection of anecdotal short stories and insights from my years as an executive in corporate America.

Specifically, I imagined writing a revolutionary business book with marketing theories and models the world had never seen. It would be required reading in the best MBA schools and I would spend my remaining days writing and lecturing on marketing (*always aim high!*).

Or, perhaps it would be a book that would enable me to share my personal stories and lessons from corporate America. In it I would discuss some of the most important lessons I learned about leadership, vision, management, and teamwork. I would wax eloquently about managing corporate expectations and delivering results. I might even share humorous tales about offsite excursions: from traveling with evening gowns on the QE2 for one company to hunting quail in snake guards for another.

But those books must wait until another time. Something happened that would make the right book, *this book*, happen right now.

I didn't choose to write this book - it chose me.

I was asked to be a speaker at an executive women's conference for 200 attendees. I was honored and pleased that they had asked me to speak. I have spoken at many conferences over the years and am very confident about my abilities. This time, though, it was different.

I had always spoken on topics I know well: marketing, brand management, consumer promotion, trade/customer marketing, advertising, marketing leadership, and so on.

This time, however, I was asked to speak on the topic of *Work/Life* Balance. This topic made me nervous because I don't consider myself an expert and therefore don't have any advice or solutions. But, I couldn't let the leaders of this conference know that! So, with an external sense of confidence I said, "Sure, I'd love to speak!"

I used all available resources.

During the course of my career I have often taken on challenges that stretched me beyond my own capabilities. In those cases I learned to go for help. Since this was another one of those occasions, I decided to use all of my available resources once again.

First, I brainstormed about my personal experience. How was it that I managed (or did I?) a career, a family, and a personal life? What were my goals? What was my support system? What choices and decisions did I have to make?

At my company, RTM&J® - Real Truth Marketing & Joy - we focus on *Marketing For Women* by providing *Total Business Marketing Solutions.* So clearly we have a lot of knowledge about women and brands. I pored through our work, reviewing it from the vantage point of executive women and the work/life balance issue.

Then, I pulled some of my favorite books, magazines and articles about women from the RTM&J® library. I reviewed our collection of marketing, biology, psychology, sociology and self-help books. My staff completed a secondary research review from the Census Bureau, AFL-CIO, Catalyst, the Bureau of Labor Statistics, The Family and Work Institute, Women Business and Professional Women USA, the General Accounting Office, and more.

Finally, and most importantly, I tapped my women's network. I called a few of the smartest and most successful women corporate executives I have ever known to ask them for their perspectives, insights, and advice.

I was overwhelmed with the support I received! These busy, successful, high ranking corporate women were willing, even eager, to set everything aside for a few minutes and talk with me about this important women's issue. They were passionate. They were phenomenal!

The project began to have a life of its own.

With only three weeks until my presentation, I found that I had tapped into something important – something that these women corporate executives wanted to know more about for themselves. *Moreover, these executives genuinely wanted to share their stories in order to help empower other women in finding their work/life balance.*

I became passionate about doing as much as I could to advance this project. I began calling more and more women asking for their input.

As I listened, I became convinced that the work/life balance issue, while very real, was only one element of a larger need. *What these women were in search of was "joy," for themselves and for other executive women.*

It was obvious that their stories needed to be shared.

I was convinced that the perspectives of these phenomenal women needed to be shared with as many others as possible. And so, what began on October 21, 2003, with my first telephone call to an executive friend, concluded with this document being sent to the publisher on October 30, 2003 – a mere eight business days later!

The process of pulling this book together is a great example of what happens to women when they become genuinely engaged and why we struggle with work/life balance issues. We become passionate about things we know to be simply the right thing to do.

Writing this book wasn't my only responsibility.

Like many women, I was committed to a few other responsibilities during those eight long days:

- *Designing a strategic approach to a quantitative research study, including analysis methods (thanks, Michele)*
- *Attending my daughter's parent-teacher conference (I'm so proud of her)*
- *Leading, designing, and managing the execution of qualitative exploratory research on creative advertising concepts (incredible responses)*
- *Removing a root canal filling for a crown (ouch!)*
- *Attending the opera (Aida – terrific!)*
- *Watching the World Series (okay, I don't like baseball, but I'm married)*
- *Investigating strategic marketing approaches for multi-cultural markets (complicated but fun!)*
- *Having my house painted (love it!)*
- *Preparing a marketing strategy presentation for 75 corporate executives (it's looking good!)*
- *Writing and delivering a 67-page brand positioning presentation for 50 corporate executives (it went well, thank you)*
- *Going on a planned weekend beach vacation with my family (Seagrove is beautiful and relaxing – so is the Internet Café and Mailboxes Etc. on 30A)*
- *Pitching two new business clients (cross your fingers)*
- *Helping my daughter with homework (absolute values inside inequalities)*
- *Dealing with a laptop LCD blowout and the one-week absence of my primary computer (this hurt beyond belief – especially writing this book using Windows 98®)*
- *Walking 15 miles (okay, not really, but it was close)*
- *Inviting and following up with my brother and his family on Thanksgiving plans (they're in Illinois)*
- *Attending a friend's birthday party (one month late due to schedule conflicts)*
- *And even more tedious stuff I won't bother you with*

As I wrote this list even I was shocked! It seems impossible that I would even try to accomplish everything. Am I crazy? On the other hand, what on the list was I willing to give up? What was I willing to live without? For most of us, including me, the answer was simple: *nothing*!

Now, let me be clear: I asked for help!

My family was terrific. Thanks to my husband of nearly 16 years, Jim, who manages everything, and I mean everything, at home. Thanks to our 13-year old daughter, Jayne, who is wonderful, a great student, and her mom's greatest supporter.

Thanks to the women in the RTM&J® family for all of their help and support, especially Michele Shaute and Karen Brethower, PhD.

A special "thank you" goes to the women who participated.

And, last but not least, very special and heartfelt thanks go to the phenomenal women corporate executives who shared their valuable time, perspectives, insights, and ideas on work/life balance so that we can all experience *joy.*

Step 1:
Get to What's Real

Get to What's Real

It is unfair to hold people responsible
for our illusions of them.
- Comtesse Diane

Remember the Broadway show tune turned television commercial where a woman boasts she can "bring home the bacon, fry it up in the pan, and never, never, never let him forget he's a man 'cause I'm a w-o-m-a-n"?

Now, many years later, women still strive to be superwomen – doing it all with perfection. Years ago many women made very difficult decisions to *either* have a family *or* a career; today's women are no longer satisfied with only these choices. And, while we want it all, we are still struggling with how to achieve it.

Women corporate executives deal with "balance" regardless of family status. Truthfully, this is not a new issue; it has been talked about and written about for many years. However, with more women reaching executive levels than ever before, the work/life balance issue is reaching a new crescendo.

For me, this crescendo hit about two years ago, shortly after September 11, 2001. My family and I decided life is short and we should be doing exactly what we want to be doing. *Now.*

I needed joy.

While I loved my 15+ years in Fortune 500 America, for some reason *joy* was always just out of reach. I always envisioned it coming with my next promotion. But promotions came and went. When I reached what I thought would be the pinnacle of my career I couldn't help but say to myself, "Is this it? Is this all there is?"

After some genuine self-searching, the real truth emerged that I knew my work better than I knew my family. Another real truth was that I had always planned on using my experience in the corporate sector to start my own company but had seen this dream slipping away as I became more comfortable with the perks of senior management.

Throughout my career I had told myself that I would work hard *now* so that I could enjoy life *later*. I told myself that as my husband is a stay-at-home dad, *our family was in balance* and therefore I didn't need to be. I told myself *I was doing the best thing for our future.*

But that was my head talking and not my heart. *Joy* was not just something I wanted, it was something I needed. And to attain it, I realized that I needed more balance: more time with my family and for me. Finally, if I was going to find *joy* in working, it had to be on my terms.

I don't regret my time as a corporate executive; in fact, I even occasionally miss it. I had the pleasure of working with some of the most talented people in the world, at the most respected companies on the planet.

Work is part of who I am. And so is my family. But so is the entrepreneurial spirit.

I have always been an entrepreneur.

I was always an entrepreneur at heart, feeling the need to create even within the walls of the corporate sector. Now it was my time to start my own company. And so I joined the more than 6 million other women entrepreneurs, founding my own company alongside the other women-owned firms that represent 28% of all U.S. businesses (source: U.S. Census 2000).

Interestingly, between 1997 and 2002, the number of women-owned firms increased by 14% nationwide, twice the rate of all firms. The greatest motivations among women for becoming entrepreneurs include: frustration with the work environment; a desire for greater challenges, and more flexibility (source: Catalyst; Center for Business Women's Research).

With *joy* as my personal and professional goal (i.e., results, balance, and enjoyment), in early spring 2002 I founded RTM&J® Inc. – Real Truth Marketing & Joy.

I continue to deal with work/life balance issues.

Some people believe that you can work whenever you want if you have your own company. They imagine coming into the office only a few days a week, just doing work they like, and working eight (or less) hours a day. And somehow, as if by magic, their company will grow, they will build a client base and will begin to turn a profit. I believe this is one reason why so many new businesses fail. While you do have more control over your time, it is simply a matter of *when* not *how much*.

For me, the idea of balance isn't an *every moment in time* idea. I once heard that marriage is never 50%-50%; it is 90%-10% or 10%-90% most of the time. On rare occasions it is 50%-50% as the scale tips back and forth. The key is to recognize this fact and strive to maintain balance over time. This is how I choose to think about work/life balance. As such, I am constantly tipping the scale, feeling the effects of being off kilter most of the time. So, this book is as much for my own benefit as it is for the women who read it.

This book is about women empowering women.

This book's objective is to empower women corporate executives in finding personal and professional *joy* through achieving work/life balance.

Why is work/life balance such an issue *now*?

The answer to this question rests in what we know about what's going on with women in general as well as understanding what goes on inside each individual woman.

At RTM&J® we monitor women's short and long term trends in order to understand what's real. These trends provide a solid foundation in order to answer the question of why the work/life balance issue among executive women is gaining momentum.

Women-Over-Time Decade Definitions™

Over the past 50 years women have continued to evolve in their social, family, and workforce roles. To summarize this evolution, RTM&J® has identified six key "decade definitions" which ultimately point us to *what's next*.

"Definition" - *Women in the 1950s:* During the 1950s women were seeking "definition," defining, accepting and perfecting their roles against cultural expectations.

Those were the days of June Clever. Socially, post-war women were striving to be perfect homemakers, wives, and mothers. Complete with new kitchen appliances and pearls, these women gave birth to the Baby Boom – the greatest number of babies in modern history.

Women were also seeking definition in the workforce. There were 18 million working women (32% of working age female population), nearly half of whom were married, who made up 29% of the workforce.

In 1952, women in the workforce could no longer be ignored. A coalition of civic groups, women's organizations, and labor and employer organizations, including the Women's Bureau, formed a *National Committee for Equal Pay* and held a national conference to discuss women's role in the work place.

In 1955, the White House Conference held the first *Effective Use of Womanpower* in which it explored sex-stereotypes as limits to opportunities for women. Women's liberation was on its way.

"Liberation" - Women in the 1960s: Political and social issues began creating cultural change. Women felt more liberated from traditional roles and responsibilities, and began exploring new models of behavior.

As women now comprised 33% of the workforce, the *President's Commission on the Status of Women* was established to investigate the role of working women. The Women's Bureau took an active role in developing studies and recommending ways to overcome sex discrimination in employment.

Two key pieces of legislation were passed during this decade. First passed was the Equal Pay Act, requiring companies to pay equal wages regardless of sex to all those performing equal tasks. Second, the Civil Rights Act was passed, which included Title VII, prohibiting firms with 15 or more employees from discriminating on the basis of sex.

A revolution was brewing, and women were leading the way.

"Revolution" - Women in the 1970s: For the first time, more than half of all women aged 16 and over were participating in the labor force. Taking a stand, women began a women's revolution.

Equal rights were at the forefront, from Billy Jean King and Bobby Riggs on the tennis court to introducing the concept of "sex discrimination" as a workplace issue.

Executive Order 12138 established a national *Policy on Women's Business Enterprise*, directing Federal agencies to establish goals for contract awards to women-owned businesses. And, the Women's Bureau director testified for an amendment to Title VII of the Civil Rights Act, banning employment discrimination based on pregnancy.

Certainly, a revolution was underway – leading the way to equality between men and women in the workplace.

"Equalization" - Women in the 1980s: "I can bring home the bacon, fry it up in the pan, and never, never, never let you forget you're a man," summarizes the "I can do anything you can do better" attitude of this decade.

Labeled the *Decade of Women* at the United Nation's 1985 World Conference, big shoulder pads and grey flannel suits and bow ties marked the masculine fashion trend, as women believed that to be respected they needed to be more like men.

With women representing the majority of college students and ultimately half of women in the workforce, they started to prove their true capabilities. Several initiatives including *Women in Nontraditional Careers (WINC), Job Training Partnership Act,* and *Emergency Math and Science Education and Jobs Act* helped bridge women into a broader career base.

In addition, the issue of Sexual Harassment came to the forefront as official guidelines were issued, reaffirming it as an unlawful employment practice.

Separately, child care emerged as the key work and family issue, with the Women's Bureau establishing employer-sponsored child-care systems as a primary initiative. During this decade, the number of child care centers exploded in the United States.

So, in the 1980s women were beginning to be taken seriously in the workforce, as equals to men in traditional non-female roles. But with that equalization, came the realization that while "I may be able to anything; I can't do everything at the same time."

"Realization" - Women in the 1990s: With 6 in 10 women participating in the labor force (vs. 7 in 10 for men), and 72% of them having children in the home, many women realized that they couldn't have it all and remain healthy.

Women began choosing lifestyles and trying to maintain balance. Flex-time and working from home became more appealing and acceptable. And in order to make themselves more comfortable, they introduced pantsuits into the workday.

Keeping in balance became more of an issue during this decade in part due to the number of women shouldering full household responsibilities. In 1999, 25% of all women over the age of 15 had never married, another 12.9% were divorced or separated, and another 10% were widowed. The result is that the percentage of women living alone rose for almost every age group, except those 65-74 where it was statistically unchanged. In addition to living alone, more families are being maintained by women without a husband. This proportion rose from 10.7% of all families in 1970 to 17.8% in 1998.

Indeed, during the 1990s women, and the world, realized that women play significant roles at home and at work. With this realization, a new flexible and relaxed corporate culture emerged. With more and more independence among women, a celebration of women was soon to come.

"Celebration" - Women in the 2000s: Finally, women came into their own with a sense of confidence and celebration.

Pink Power ruled and *You Go Girl!* was the motto during this decade which tipped the scale on so many demographic indicators.

For the first time, educational attainment among ages 18-24 tipped to women – with women holding 58% of bachelor's degrees or higher. Even among those over 25 years of age, women held the majority of bachelor's and master's degrees (source: Census 2000 QT-P20).

Although better educated, women earned less than their male counterparts: (1) Professional degrees $55.4k vs. $90.6k (2) Bachelor's degrees $35.4k vs. $49.9k (source: Census 2000). With 21% of wives having attained higher levels of education than their husbands, only 15% of wives earned at least $5k more than their husbands, and in unmarried-partner households that proportion is 22%.

During this decade women changed their lifestyles to accommodate their place in the workforce. For example, women in 2001 waited nearly five more years to get married verses 1970. The average number of children born to women decreased from 3 in 1980 to 1.9 in 2001. And finally, nearly twice as many, 19% verses 10%, of women were childless in 2001 verses 1980.

Celebrating the point that they no longer need to prove themselves to be the *same as men*, women became comfortable that they were *different but equal.* Women also began networking with other women, unifying in support of themselves and others.

"Unification" - Women Moving Forward: Today, women are aligning with other women, building powerful and supportive networks. This is the decade of *women empowering women.*

Today's movement has nothing to do with men. It is not "anti-men" or "militant" or anything less than truly feminine. Today it is about women.

Working long hours, today's women contribute a majority of their families' incomes. And it doesn't matter your family or marital status.

Married and unmarried women receive similar pay and work similar hours. Women with children under age 18 who live at home work roughly the same number of hours as women without children and earn similar portions of their families' incomes (source: AFL-CIO). As a whole, working women are facing increasing household responsibility and dealing with many similar issues of work/life balance.

Women are unified in their views of corporate America, with more than 90% of working women of all ages and races supporting stronger laws to constrain corporate America such as stronger equal pay laws and stronger laws to challenge discrimination (source: AFL-CIO).

Working women are unified in what they believe are important workplace benefits, with more than half stating the following as "very important:" secure, affordable health insurance; prescription drug coverage; equal pay; paid sick leave; retirement benefits; paid vacation time, and; paid family leave. Further, nearly 80% of working women say that child care options and flex hours are important benefits that are lacking in their current companies (source: AFL-CIO).

Overall, women are becoming unified while at the same time more accepting of the range of roles and responsibilities that women choose to adopt. Generally, women are empowering other women for success – however each woman might define that for themselves.

Real Time Summary

Women's lives have changed.

Women's lives have changed both professionally and personally. Overall, their lives have become less stable and more complex resulting in the need for an expanded support network.

To compound this complexity, their world has changed at the office as well. Economic issues combined with morphing competitive landscapes and increased expectations has led to a hectic, ad-hoc, day-to-day rush to business results.

The predictable corporate planning cycle is dead.

A mere ten years ago, an executive could count on working long and difficult days primarily during the planning season and perhaps at year's end.

With the traditional annual planning and execution cycle shifting to real time planning and execution, "crazy hours" have become the norm. And for many, there doesn't seem to be a light at the end of the tunnel.

Life at home still depends on her.

On the personal front, women have more to do than ever. The number of women living in non-traditional families continues to rise and women are picking up enhanced responsibilities.

Even within traditional family settings, the redistribution of home responsibilities is more a myth than a true reality. While men may be spending a few more hours a week helping around the house, women still bear the brunt of the overall accountability for home and family life. Who is responsible for decorating the home? Buying the family greeting cards? You got it.

Women strive for rejuvenation.

At the same time, women are finding they need time for self-rejuvenation and social belonging. Again, for many, this doesn't seem to be a realistic or achievable goal given the demands of daily life. How many brands can you name that talk about rejuvenation and renewal?

Work/life balance issues are gaining momentum in part because women are recognizing that they desire and deserve solutions that are tailored to them.

At RTM&J® we believe that every brand has an inherent real truth that will connect with the hearts, minds, and behaviors of women. And as a result of that connection, everyone involved will experience the joy of successful results, stronger brands, and enhanced consumer loyalty.

We have listened to hundreds of women talk about how they think, what they feel, and what they do – on every topic from new products and shopping experiences to cultural issues and entertainment. Moreover, we've heard them talk about themselves. If we counted our entire professional experience, the numbers would reach into the thousands!

During interviews with Women Corporate Executives for this book, the basics of Think-Feel-Do™ proved true once more.

What Women Say

RTM&J® conducted an online quantitative study among women corporate executives to determine what women think, feel, and do regarding work/life balance.

Now, in all honesty, it wasn't executed among a blind sample as my quantitative team would have preferred. Instead, we forwarded the survey to the RTM&J® database of executive women as well as to the conference attendees of the Fortune 500 client for which I was preparing my keynote. We even suggested that they send the survey on to other executive women that they knew. By our counts, about 200 women were invited to participate in the survey of which 55 responded (28%). Of these, about one-third came from a cross section of one Fortune 500 client company.

The women represented virtually all incomes, ages, as well as work and home situations.

Although a strong range of demographic indicators were reported, the majority of the women were between the ages of 35-54, approximately a third had incomes between $50k-$99k, more than half worked in full time in a large corporate setting, and were nearly equally balanced regarding their home and family situation:

Balance Survey Quantitative Research Sample

Age	%	Income	%
21-34	29	0-$49k	12
35-54	64	$50k-$99k	36
55+	7	$100k-149k	16
		$150k-$200k	15
		$200k+	20

Work Situation	%
Full Time Home Office	11
Full Time – Small Business Setting	16
Full Time – Large Corporation Setting	58
Part Time	5
Other	7

Home Situation	%
Single/Divorced – live alone	24
Single/Divorced – live with child(ren)	7
Single/Divorced – have roommate	4
Married/Significant Other – no kids	20
Married/Significant Other – kids in home	36
Married/Significant Other – empty nester	9

The women have support for pursuing careers and help maintaining work/life balance.

Overwhelmingly, the women agree they have support from their spouse/significant other (80%), their children (89%), extended family (83%) in their career endeavors. In addition, most (69%) of the women have a support network of people who help them through work/life balance issues.

At work, however, they feel a lack of support. Only 20% of the women have dedicated assistants or secretaries, 46% share support staff with others, and 35% have no administrative support staff at all. Nearly 50% have no employees directly reporting to them. And, while the vast majority (93%) says they are compassionate with colleagues when they share balance issues with them, only 20% strongly agree they openly discuss their issues with their colleagues.

So while these women feel emotional support from their friends and family, often they feel like they are going at it alone – especially in the workplace.

The women are shouldering virtually all of the household responsibilities – from providing financial support to being the primary caregiver and homemaker.

Although not believing that it's a woman's job to be the primary caregiver/homemaker, the vast majority of these women take on this role. Among the 69% of the women responders who have a spouse or significant other in the home, 79% disagree that it is a woman's job to be the primary caregiver/homemaker.

However, 83% of the women carry the primary or substantive role in providing these responsibilities. When asked how often they were the person performing the following tasks in the household, it is clear that women still provide the primary caregiver/homemaker role (percent responding "always" or "frequently" verses "seldom" or "never"):

Percent of Women Corporate Executives
Agreeing they are the Person Performing
Household Tasks

Task	%
Buying/Sending Cards/Gifts	97
Managing Social Calendar	96
Shopping for Clothes	94
Planning Holiday Celebrations/Meals	93
Planning Vacations	93
Cooking/Preparing Meals	87
Shopping for Food	80
Doing Laundry	76
Planning/Managing Finances/Investments	66
Paying Household Bills	64
Managing/Doing HH Repairs/Maintenance	*40*
Mowing/Yard work	*13*

Among those who have children in the home...

Attending School Functions	100
Disciplining	100
Managing Extracurricular Activities	91
Arranging Childcare	84

Adding to their overall sense of responsibility, these women are also significant financial contributors to their households. Nearly 51% of the women are "the primary financial providers" to their household, while another 42% are "substantial" financial providers. Only 7.2% responded that they "contribute" to the financial status of their household or that that their income has "little to do" with their household financial status.

With carrying the primary financial, homemaker, and caregiver responsibilities for their households, it's no wonder that these women say the balance issue is important. And, it's no surprise that 35% of the women with spouses and children in the home strongly agreed that that often argue with their spouses regarding balance issues.

The presence of children in the home increases the work/life balance issue for these women.

Not surprisingly, the demographics of women with children in the home (WWC) verses those women without children in the home (WWOC) are somewhat different. As we will be comparing our findings by these two segments it is important to provide the statistics. Generally, compared to WWOC, WWC are older, more affluent, and operate in a broader range of business settings:

	WWC %	WWOC %
Age		
21-34	12	**48**
35-54	**88**	**41**
55+	0	11
Income		
0-$49k	20	7
$50k-$99k	28	**48**
$100k-$149k	8	**26**
$150k-$200k	**20**	7
$200k+	**24**	11
Work Situation		
FT Home Office	12	3
FT Small Business	24	11
FT Large Corporation	48	**74**
Other	16	11

Overwhelmingly, the majority of the women agreed that achieving balance is a priority (95%), that balance is an important issue for me (93%), and that they personally have a work/life balance issue (57%).

WWC, however, seem to be struggling more than WWOC – and doing so in silent desperation. WWC are 6-times more likely than WWOC to *strongly* agree (44% vs. 7%) that they have a work/life balance issue.

The good news is that most of these women (69%) have a plan to achieve work/life balance. However, it seems that WWC are less structured than WWOC, 60% verses 74% respectively, saying they have a plan developed.

Don't ask; don't tell.

WWC are less than half as likely as WWOC to discuss their balance issue openly with work management (24% vs. 52%). Sixty-four percent of WWC don't discuss their balance issues with management because they fear negative consequences, verses only 37% of WWOC feeling such ramifications. Further, 44% of WWC, verses only 23% of WWOC, are concerned that their management will think that they aren't good at their job if they discuss their balance issues with them.

WWC are more likely to frequently justify unhealthy work behaviors in order to accomplish everything they need to accomplish verses WWOC, 40% verses 11% respectively. And it shows as nearly double the number (72% verses 37%) of WWC often do hours of work at home on week nights and weekends than do WWOC.

So, clearly women with children want to know - when is it my time?

Seventy-two percent of WWC *disagree* that they often schedule time just for themselves while a full 78% of WWOC *agree*! It isn't surprising that WWC are 7-times more likely (52% vs. 7%) to strongly agree that they feel they never have time for themselves.

Women are passionate about what they do – both at home and at work – especially if they have children in the home.

Overall, 82% of the women surveyed strongly or mildly agree that they love to work while 94% said they love to be at home. And, therein lays the dilemma - how to be that passionate in two different, sometimes opposing worlds?

Although an overall two-thirds of the women take their role at work very seriously, WWC verses WWOC are much more apt to *strongly* agree with this fact (76% vs. 52%).

Not only do WWC take their work more seriously, they also claim to be even more committed to work than WWOC. When surveyed, 48% of WWC, verses only 26% of WWOC, *strongly* agree that they "love to work." This may in part be due to women who do not *love to work* having left the workforce and therefore not included in the survey sample.

Being home is also more important to WWCs, with 68% strongly agreeing that they love to be at home verses only 48% of WWOCs.

Women corporate executives agree – they need a wife! Seriously, a stay-at-home househusband would be just fine with them.

Yes, these women love to work. Nearly two-thirds admit having aggressive career aspirations. Moreover, they love it so much that 73% do *not* want someone who would support them financially so that they could stop working. In fact, overwhelmingly they say just the opposite!

Nearly 80% agreed that *they* would support a spouse/significant other to stay at home and do the majority of the household responsibilities. Further, WWC are even more adamant about this than WWOC, as 68% verses 22% respectively *strongly* agree that this is something they would do!

Women believe that they must perform better than men at work to obtain the same level of respect.

Overwhelmingly, 78% of the women say that women have to perform better at work than men to obtain the same level of respect. Interestingly, there were no significant differences among demographic segments of those who disagreed to those who agreed with this statement.

Women ThinkFeelDo™

ThinkFeelDo™ is a customized, proprietary way of interpreting how consumers perceive, internalize, and act on stimuli in the marketplace. During the course of writing this book ThinkFeelDo™ proved to be on-target once again. The aforementioned quantitative research is reported in the ThinkFeelDo™ boxes below.

1. Think

Women Think	
Less "What I Do"	*More "Who I Am"*
Sequential	Simultaneous
Compartments	Holistic
Structure	Balance
Seek Differences	Seek Similarities
Status	Best
Good Enough	Perfect

He thinks of conquering work/life balance as "something he does."

I interviewed men on the topic of work/life balance and found that they were not immune to the issue. They face it; however, it seems in black and white terms. Our qualitative and secondary research supports the finding that these men take structured approaches, placing rules around a situation in order to conquer it. It is this same approach that I found these men use to overcome balance issue.

For him, it is work or life.

Overall, the men have a tendency to talk about work *or* life. "I have a mental code to keep work and personal life separate," says one man, while "I keep different friend sets, never socializing with my friends at work," says another.

While some women talk about creating structure and division lines, generally it is not stated as something they do naturally; it is a necessity they came to with much deliberation and maintained with considerable effort.

For him, balance is something they faced at one point in time.

On the other hand, men see clear distinctions, in black or white terms. Their prevailing theme is: do work *or* life - each in its own time. He does his best at each and if he isn't perfect, so be it: it is good enough. Men speak about a *point in time* early in their careers when they faced an issue, made a decision, and moved on. For them, it is all about what they do.

On the other hand, she thinks about how dealing with balance defines "Who I Am."

When interviewing women, I tapped into a passionate connection to the issue of work/life balance. But unlike men, women see the issue as very complex, with gray tones and no clear division lines.

For her, it is work and life.

Women generally speak about work *and* life as both being a part of *who they are*. They *choose* to integrate their work and life – most often running both scenarios simultaneously in their hearts and brains throughout their day and life.

Unable or unwilling to compartmentalize and let one side "win," many of the women take a more holistic approach, striving to find the relationships and searching for the connections between work and life in order to maximize their role in each.

For her, achieving balance is an ongoing and evolving issue.

The women talk about achieving balance as being an *ongoing and evolving process* that they deal with on an everyday basis. A single "point in time" decision that resolves matters once and for all does not seem realistic or reasonable to them.

And, finally, women believe that their situation is somewhat unique. They feel they need to find the solution that allows them to be perfect at everything. For her, it's about how *work and life* define *who I am*.

Women may struggle more than men with work/life balance issues in part because they view it as part of *who they are* verses *something they do*.

2. Feel

Women Feel	
Less "It's Business"	*More "It's Personal"*
Efficient	Productive
Transactions Matter	Relationships Matter
In-Charge	Involved
Me	Us
Want to Feel Right	Want to Feel Validated

He feels dealing with work/life balance issues is just business.

On the topic of work/life balance, the men I interviewed talked mostly about how the decisions they had made put them in charge of their lives. They share examples that prove that their decisions were smart and *right for themselves* (verses the women who primarily discuss how it was working for everyone else and only sometimes for themselves).

For example, one successful male corporate executive declared, "I try to get out everyday in time to be home for dinner; it's not a huge issue. It has never come up on a personnel review."

For him, it was just a simple black and white decision.

The men speak about the work/life issue as a simple transaction. "I work when I am there and then I leave and prioritize my family." For him, it is just another business decision.

She feels it's really personal.

In contrast, I found the women executives to be inextricably involved with both their work and their families. Indeed, they feel a tense relationship with each. They believe that both require their full presence and their support. And they want to make sure they do the right thing for everyone, in both places.

Women feel special at home and at work.

I found that one of the reasons the work/life balance issue is so difficult for women is that both work and life make them feel special, yet in different ways. They are involved deeply in both relationships.

Interestingly, each woman with whom I spoke validated her rationale for working, although the question was never asked. For her, it was always a personal matter and one full of feeling.

3. Do

Women Do	
Less "Compete with Others"	*More "Compete with Time"*
Win	Positive Experience
On/Off Switch	1-10 Dial
Master Complexity	Embrace Simplicity
Challenge/Conflict	Harmony
Independence	Interdependence

He competes with others and wants to win.

The men seem to have an off/on switch that helps them navigate between work and home. They aren't concerned about any potential conflict that may be an outcome of their decisions. Generally, they see the issue, conquer it, and move on without second guessing, feeling guilty, or wondering how it was perceived by others.

She competes with time and tries to survive.

Many of the women have a hard time flipping their work/life switch on and off. They have a dial instead, which they constantly spin to the specific magnitude and area of their life to which they must respond at any given time.

Many of the women who participated in this project want everything around them to work together in a harmonious way. And they dwell on it, feeling guilty (or trying not to), when it doesn't. They look for a simple answer, although recognizing the challenge and suspecting that it is not readily going to be apparent.

Generally, she feels interdependent and fully integrated. She competes with time, trying to fit it all in, yet rarely succeeds.

Get to What's Real

In summary, women's work/life balance issues are real. This book explores these issues from many different women's viewpoints and offers suggestions regarding how to achieve joy through attaining work/life balance.

GET TO WHAT'S REAL
CHOOSE WHAT IS REAL FOR YOU:

I:

- ❑ *need joy*
- ❑ *continue to struggle with work/life balance*
- ❑ *want to empower myself and other women by unifying powerful and supportive networks*

I believe that:

- ❑ *women can make it better*
- ❑ *women lead complicated lives*
- ❑ *women are equal but different*
- ❑ *joy is important*
- ❑ *I am reconsidering my life*

I am ready to:

- ❑ *evaluate and assess what I think, how I feel, and what I will do to create joy and achieve work/life balance*

Notes:

Step 2:
Figure Out the Truth

Figure Out the Truth

You never find yourself until you face the truth.
- Pearl Bailey

Overwhelmingly, laughter was the first response from women corporate executives when I asked them to share their perspectives, insights, and advice on the work/life balance issue for my presentation and this book.

What, are you kidding?

Then, a long pause would follow. Surely I had called them by mistake. "What, are you kidding? There is no such thing! I don't think I'm the appropriate person to speak on this topic." Inevitably, they would say that they knew other women who managed balancing work and life better than they did. None saw themselves as a role model.

Although every woman I spoke with admitted to having a work/life balance issue, I could sense an undertone that they were feeling embarrassed and perhaps somewhat guilty for not having "the solution." After all, they were some of the most successful, most respected women in the field of business. They had proven their capabilities – except now they were being "out-ed" as closet life/work balance strugglers.

After I assured them that I wasn't expecting a magic answer, finally, very slowly, they began to talk. I found them to be refreshingly open and candid.

Their perspectives fell into three areas: logical ways in which they thought about the issue; emotional feelings they were experiencing because of the issue; and what they were doing to manage the issue both for themselves and for other women.

Women corporate executives speak out.

What I liked best about collecting women's perspectives, insights, and ideas was that each one had something unique to say which added value to this project.

One of my bosses once said to me, "If you can come out of any experience with three new relevant ideas, it's been a good experience."

My hope is that by reading the words of other executive women you will find at least three perspectives, insights, and ideas that resonate for you, thereby helping you in your search for joy.

I hope you enjoy as much as I do the perspectives, insights, and ideas presented by these extraordinary women corporate executives. From middle management to the top posts, I asked these women three basic questions: (1) Do you have a work/life balance issue? Or, would you characterize it another way; (2) If so, what do you think about it, how does it make you feel, and what are you doing about it, and (3) do you have any perspectives, insights, or ideas to share with other women?

The response was tremendous.

Nearly 75% of the women I reached out to chose to participate. In some cases the remaining wished to participate but had company policies that either prohibited interviews or required approval processes that interfered with their participation. Others had scheduling conflicts (remember this whole project took a total of eight days from conceiving the idea to sending this document to publication).

I spent between ten and thirty minutes on the telephone with each woman. Following the interview, I transcribed my notes and sent them their stories for final approval. In a few cases, the women emailed me their stories directly without a telephone interview.

Please note that I have added in a few things to their comments.

First, at the beginning of each woman's section, I added *section titles and subtitles* as well as *an introduction to each interviewee from my perspective.* At the end of each section I added *Choose Your Commitments*, and *Notes*.

Following each woman's story, you may wish to check the boxes that you are willing to try in order to achieve balance in your life. We'll revisit them again in more detail during Step 3: Plan for Joy and Balance.

What's Your Story?

Women Corporate Executives Speak Out In Their Own Words

In the following pages are the perspectives, insights, and ideas from Women Corporate Executives. These women were refreshingly open, candid, and forthcoming in their characterization of their work/life balance issues. As such, they are role models for strength, courage, and leadership in speaking out on this very complex topic. Indeed, these personal characteristics undoubtedly supported their rise to some of the top posts in the corporate world.

I've chosen to lead the series with an anomaly.

While the first story is more emotionally raw than the rest, its undercurrents were heard in many of the subsequent interviews.

Specifically, the first entry, "Nobody Knows," is from a woman who wanted desperately to participate but was fearful of the possible negative career repercussions if she did. Her words were so genuine, her voice so clear, and her heart so heavy that I talked her into letting me print her story anonymously with only a general company industry subhead. She was taking no chances.

This is the only interviewee who asked to be kept anonymous. *My introductions are in italics before each entry.*

From the dark, her voice is heard.

<u>*Nobody Knows*</u>

Senior Vice President, General Manager
Apparel Company

While interviewing someone else for this book, she said to me, "Rhonda, you should call [name], she's handling it all – children and senior-level accountability. I'm sure she'd have a lot of advice." I called her that evening, introduced myself, and listened as she didn't want to tell me the things she was saying.

It is harder than anyone knows or admits.

I can't believe you are getting women to talk about their work/life balance issues. How do they even find ten minutes to talk with you? They must be lying; how would they deal with the career repercussions if they told you the truth?

I have to create a face.

I can't take the risk of letting my company know that I struggle with anything let alone something as big and female as work/life balance. They will think that I am not a good manager, that I can't handle my responsibilities. It will make me look weak and fragile which is not acceptable.

I have to create a face that I know exactly what I'm doing, that I don't have any problems meeting their expectations and my own. They have to believe it. I can't be seen looking vulnerable; there are people eyeing my job and they'll smell blood.

Nobody knows the scrutiny I feel.

I don't know if you can truly understand the balance issue unless you're a woman, especially one with kids and the primary responsibility for them.

My industry is male dominated and most of the women are single, have quit, or are doing what I'm doing -- hiding their difficulties. I'm always aware of the scrutiny being placed on me as a working woman. I can't flinch. I know what they're thinking – they're just waiting for me to fail. Many women do; I'm trying hard not to.

My home life is suffering.

I love my family and I try my best to be there for them. Given that I work insane office hours, I spend my off-work time focusing on my children because they are young and really need me. I stay strong for them and don't let them know how tired I am.

Unfortunately, my husband takes the brunt of my misery. He's the one that is left out in the cold. I'm hoping that someday when the children are older and can do more for themselves that he and I will reconnect. For now, we just have to manage to get through it. He respects and supports what I do: it is just hard on all of us. I'm afraid, though, that all of this might take its toll on my marriage.

I really do love working.

I know that my life must sound awful, but I really do like my job. I'm not complaining about my accountability, my responsibility, or my company's expectations. I am successful at driving the bottom line and am proud of my accomplishments. I have worked hard in my career and have reaped the rewards of climbing the ladder. I'm driven and good at my job.

I'm just not allowed to have any issues.

My company talks a good game, but that's all it is. I can read between the lines. Their actions don't measure up. When I had my children I could sense their distrust. I just kept waiting to be fired or shoved off to a lesser responsibility once I returned from maternity leave.

I need to get off the phone now: I need to get the kids to bed.

Good luck.

CHOOSE YOUR COMMITMENTS

I will:
- ❑ *Be honest with myself and with others*
- ❑ *Not hide behind a face but face it head on*
- ❑ *Be confident and demand/ trust that I have the respect I deserve, or go somewhere else*

Respect Diversity

Julie Reid
Assistant Vice President, Strategy & Research
Washington Mutual

I've known Julie for years and had the pleasure of working with her for some of them. She's an intelligent, bright and dedicated young executive who is learning how to build a life while she pursues a career.

My company, Washington Mutual, has been voted as one of the best places for women to work because of its work/life balance policies. I'm not sure I want to leave at 5:00pm, although it is company policy. I really love to work and when I "get in the zone" it is hard for me to stop and leave. On the other hand, sometimes I feel that it isn't accepted for me to enjoy the company policy.

Work / life balance is important for men and women.

Valuing diversity is a core belief at Washington Mutual, so we benefit from having a strong female presence in leadership and management. This has led to the development of policies that reflect the needs its employees who wish to have more balance in their lives.

But it isn't just the women championing this idea. We also have a significant male presence that is dedicated to pursuing balance for themselves and their families.

However, there seems to be an understood, yet unstated, view of traditional values and family traditions.

I completely respect my colleagues with spouses and children. I understand and empathize with their desires to coach their children's baseball teams, take them to dance classes, and attend their recitals. Everyone is supportive of these moms and dads making sure they leave at 5:00pm to have time with their families.

As a single woman, I know what it feels like to be responsible for all of the shopping, cooking, cleaning, and laundry. I also like to schedule time for me, my friends, and my family. However, I don't feel the same level of support from my peers for leaving at 5:00pm to do these things.

I get the feeling that they believe my leaving work unfinished at 5:00pm is selfish, that my needs aren't as important as those with spouses and/or children. It's almost like they say that they would be happy to stay, they just can't. Sometime I feel guilty, and then I wonder if they would really stay.

Sometimes I feel that as a single woman, my colleagues assume that I'll stay late to get things done.

I've begun to notice that I'm asked to accept more work and last minute tasks because of my perceived ability to be more flexible in my work hours. While it is great to be valued and respected for my abilities, there appears to be a subtle lack of value and respect for my lifestyle.

My willingness to be a team player is beginning to have consequences in my personal life. The man I've been dating for nearly a year feels resentful about my time at work. He complains about the hours I work and my resulting lack of time for him. This is becoming a regular thread to my life.

Now in my 30s, I need to make time for me – in order to establish the life I want.

Women have made great strides in establishing business credibility and I have been a beneficiary of their years of struggle. I too have struggled and worked to achieve my level of success. And, I don't mind a bit. As I said before, I love to work. It is part of who I am. However, it is not all that I am.

Whether it is real or perceived, I believe that everyone, regardless of their lifestyle, should be supported in pursuing the career they choose and the life they want.

CHOOSE YOUR COMMITMENTS

I will:

- ❑ *Take advantage of my company benefits*
- ❑ *Continue to support others in their work/life balance pursuits*
- ❑ *Give myself permission to pursue my career and my life with equal passion and commitment*

Notes:

<u>*Do As I Say, Not As I Do*</u>

Jaime Scholl
Brand Manager
The Sanford Company

I've known Jaime for years and she is on the fast track. Smart, articulate, and motivated, she can handle just about anything. When it comes to work/life balance, though, she's struggling along with everyone else.

Life often takes a back seat.

Unfortunately, I often find that my "life" takes a back seat to my "work." It is not something that I am proud of, but something that is quite true.

There are so many complexities to life, so many unaccounted variables that achieving a sense of control over one's life is next to impossible. However, control over one's work is manageable.

Several things contribute to my work-over-life imbalance.

I believe that there are three contributing factors that drive me to sacrifice my life for my work.

First, my single status and living arrangements lead me to work longer hours than I should.

With no significant other to see after work and no roommates to come home to, I find myself rationalizing that staying longer hours at work is completely acceptable.

Why not work late, for when I do go home I end up reheating leftovers and simply watching TV until I fall asleep. When comparing the possibility that extra work could lead to upward mobility for my career or recognition for my accomplishments against reheated pasta and primetime reruns, there is a clear winner every time.

Second, the fact that I am not married and don't have any children makes it less acceptable to allow personal commitments to interfere with work, even when that work is after normal business hours.

It is far less acceptable for a single employee to not work late on account of a date or a social gathering with friends as it is acceptable for a married/parent employee to not work late on account of family obligations. It quickly becomes a judgment as to whose personal commitments are more important than another's.

It appears to be an unwritten rule that work should come before friends but not before family. Yet when your friends become your support system in the absence of a family, single employees must still choose work over friends.

Third, my petite stature and soft voice are often initially mistaken for immaturity and a lack of credibility in my workplace.

Feeling a need to overcompensate and prove my worthiness to my colleagues often leads me put in extra hours at work to demonstrate that I am focused, serious and dedicated. Likewise, the fact that I am a complete perfectionist should not be ruled out as the basis for my drive to work insane hours.

I don't know how to separate my personal needs from my personal goals.

I would love to achieve a sense of balance in my life but mostly I blame my inability to maintain a work/life balance on the fact that I just don't know how to separate my personal needs from my professional goals.

In the back of my mind I cannot help but think that now is the time to dedicate myself to my career and once I get married and have kids that my priorities will shift. However, as with most things in life, there will always be some excuse for justifying my own behavior to myself.

How do I change a "live to work" internal drive?

So, if I have any advice to give it would be: *do as I say, not as I do.* Probably not what you were looking for! I guess I fall into the category of women who need insights and advice on how to change an internal drive to *live to work* rather than *work to live.*

CHOOSE YOUR COMMITMENTS

I will:

- ❑ *Make balance a priority*
- ❑ *Trust others to believe my capabilities*
- ❑ *Stop justifying unhealthy behavior*

Notes:

Respect Yourself

Ellen Dracos
Vice President of Marketing
The Home Depot

At a hectic retailer's pace, Ellen is always challenged to find the time to talk (ask Dottie, her admin!) but found the time to provide some very insightful words about the need for self-respect.

It takes self-respect.

How do I manage life and work? I set clear boundaries and schedule time to take care of myself. It takes true self-respect and dedication to achieve it.

Learn to say "no."

I've learned to say "no" and not feel guilty about it - whether to my boss, team or family. I am crystal clear on my intentions and then I go ahead and take care of myself.

It was a hard, disillusioning lesson to learn that if I don't take care of myself, no one else will.

CHOOSE YOUR COMMITMENTS

I will:

☐ *Respect myself*
☐ *Set clear boundaries*
☐ *Schedule time for myself*
☐ *Say "no" without feeling guilty*

Listen to Yourself

Cheryl Barre
President
Russell Athleticwear Women's Division

Cheryl is one of those women who makes you ask "How does she do it?" Three kids, a demanding job, and still she has time to give herself to others. I made an appointment with her administrative assistant and called her as scheduled. She was ready. She was passionate. She had something to say.

Balance is every woman's issue.

Balance is an issue for every woman I have come into contact with and it makes no difference if she is single, married, or has children. Personally, I think about it a lot.

When I think of balance, a visual of a scale appears in my mind. And when one side dips a little, I know it is time for me to take very tangible and literal steps to get it back in balance.

To me, work is life but family is more important.

I've always thought it interesting, however, that we choose to call the sides of the scale "work" and "life." To me work is life; it is central to who I am and what I do.

In any event, balance is an important issue – one that I have lived with for some time. Without question, family is more important to me. When I get sucked up in working I find myself unhappy and I immediately take steps to get back in balance. Ultimately, I have to listen to myself in order to make the right decisions for me.

Making trade-offs has made all the difference.

I have made two important trade-offs in my career, both during my fifteen years at Pepsi. To provide more support to my two children who were then of pre-school age, I chose to work four days a week. That allowed me to be home with them during my day off and it gave me great joy and peace of mind.

Today, my children are wonderful human beings who are and will continue to make major contributions. Later, my third child (now 5) was born. I was in a very demanding senior role and came to the very difficult decision to leave it to achieve more balance in my life. And that choice is one that has brought me great personal satisfaction and fulfillment.

We need to do more to help.

Each of us, as well as corporations in general, needs to do much, much more to help women address the work/life balance issue. Personally, I have begun mentoring women. Also, within my company, I support flexibility – valuing the performance and deliverables and not just the time spent in the office.

If we all do the right thing by listening to and supporting women, we will have happy, healthy, motivated employees who are loyal and productive. And that's what it is all about.

CHOOSE YOUR COMMITMENTS

I will:

- ❑ **Listen to myself**
- ❑ **Understand what I need**
- ❑ **Choose to make tradeoffs**
- ❑ **Help other women**
- ❑ **Adjust my life as I go along**

Notes:

Know Who You Are

Karen Gullett
Vice President Brand Management
Visa International

Karen and I met at a conference where we were both panelists presenting on global brand management. That was nearly five years ago but it didn't stop Karen from returning my call. She was at an offsite meeting in London and I was getting ready for an evening of consumer research. We struggled through the cell phone static, but we reconnected!

Work brings satisfaction, but love nurtures our souls.

Balance is a very important issue and in some ways most relevant to successful women executives. In my experience, career women enjoy and find a great deal of personal satisfaction with their work, and that's why they work so hard.

That being said, fundamental to our souls is the need to be nurtured by – and to nurture - one's family, friends and inner selves. When we feel that either the professional or personal dimension is out of skew, we suffer.

The million-dollar question then is how do we achieve this balance without constantly flipping from one side to the other?

Working and being a mom made me better at both.

My daughter is now nine years old and I have worked during most of that time. She is the shine in my eyes, the spark in my heart. While it has been difficult to work at times, I felt it important that I be a good role model for her, demonstrating the capabilities of women outside the home as well as inside the home. Also, it was important to me that I defined myself not only through her but also on my own terms.

In many ways having a child made me more productive at work. Because I had more responsibilities outside of work, and indeed just simply wanted to get home to be with my family, I became more disciplined at work. For that matter, it made me more organized at home as well. Fundamentally, it made me focus on what was important and be more productive.

Keep things in perspective and know who you are.

There are several things I try to keep in mind as I manage the balance issue. First, I don't take myself too seriously. Whether I am in my role at work or at home, I try to keep things in perspective and recognize that I can't be perfect -- I can't do it all. And, I take time for me.

It is important that you get in touch with who you are. I know that I am an introvert who turns inward for rejuvenation. Without structuring time for personal self-reflection and introspection, I find that I am not refueled with the energy necessary for keeping things in balance. For example: reading, journal writing, and the rigorous practice of Yoga are essential to my life.

Is the struggle worth the aspiration?

Much has been written lately about women achieving the top spots in Fortune 500 companies only for them to wonder if it was worth the aspiration. While men may seek the top in search of authority and title, it seems women aspire to it for the process, relationships, and the outcome of a job well done. Given these different needs, is it any wonder that women are having balance issues?

Every woman is different. Take the time to get to know yourself and what you need. Don't obsess over the small stuff. And try out different techniques to help you achieve a balance that works for you. I have found these things help make work and life truly worth the aspiration!

<u>CHOOSE YOUR COMMITMENTS</u>

I will:

- ❑ **Know who I am**
- ❑ **Be more disciplined**
- ❑ **Not take myself too seriously**
- ❑ **Take time to rejuvenate myself**
- ❑ **Not obsess over the small stuff**
- ❑ **Try different techniques**

Notes:

Cherish the Little Things

Tammy Gustafson
Director of Sales
Universal Orlando

Tammy was thrilled to be a part of this project. She told me that she discussed it with her husband for days before our interview. She lamented over what she would say, but then she realized it all boiled down to family.

Work/life balance took on a whole new meaning after I had my son.

I would be lying if I told you that I had it all figured out. Clearly, I don't. But when I think about how I deal with the pressures of work and handling my responsibilities to myself and my family, it comes down to cherishing the little things.

Our daily routines help me balance.

Let me take you through a normal day in our household. My husband is usually the first one up and out of the house as he goes into work early. I wake up our 2 ½ year old and let him pick out his own clothes and put them on. I used to worry about his mismatched outfits, striped pants and polka dotted shirts. But, I've learned that it really doesn't matter, that it is easier on all of us if I delegate that responsibility to him.

We each grab a banana and a vitamin for the road, making sure we have everything we need for the day: presentation; Halloween goodie bags; laptop; and, check for the daycare. And with that, we're on our 40-minute commute to be at work and daycare before 9:00am.

My company has a daycare partnership that makes my life so much easier.

Less than a mile away from my office is my son's daycare center. Universal's Human Resources team has partnered with the center and provided discounts and curriculum input for its employees. I feel so fortunate to have this as a resource. In addition to never missing a special event, I even sneak away sometimes and have lunch with him!

My son actually eats more nutritionally there than he would if he were home! I generally don't leave work until 7:00-8:00 and the center provides him a fantastic dinner. On the way home I finish my business calls (cell phones were a great invention!) and then, *more importantly*, sing songs with him all the way home! I'm positive he's going to become a country western star!

Evenings and weekends are special times when even the routine, mundane errands are a source of joy.

Once we all return home from our day at the office and day care, we focus on each other. We give our son a bath, put on his pajamas, and let him stay up late with us so that we have family time.

Weekends are very special. We do everything together. We wake up and have a lingering breakfast. We do our errands, from grocery shopping to going to the post office, as a family. It is our time together and we make it fun. We also have horses, so we find ourselves riding our stresses away!

CHOOSE YOUR COMMITMENTS

I will:

- ❑ *Cherish the small things*
- ❑ *Take advantage of the benefits I have available*
- ❑ *Make the most of the time I have available*
- ❑ *Transform the mundane into fun*

Notes:

Be Realistic

Bonnie Carlson
Senior Vice President, Integrated Marketing
Conagra Foods

Bonnie's first response to being interviewed on the topic of work/life balance was, "I'm not sure I'm a good source for this topic, I don't have a lot of balance." Bonnie has been my mentor for many years and her words below remind me why.

Achieving balance is more idealistic than realistic.

While achieving work/life balance is an admirable goal, it is more idealistic than realistic. It is important that you declare your goals in life and are realistic about your career aspirations.

Most senior executive women that I know have made conscious choices and sacrifices. They have learned that while they may want to have the best of all worlds, it simply isn't possible.

For instance, like many married senior executive men, their spouses stay home and take care of household and family matters. In these types of jobs it is difficult, if not impossible, to think you can do it all.

In my experience corporations have high expectations. For advancement opportunities, they look for employees who are focused as well as goal and achievement oriented.

I work hard and play hard.

Personally, I receive great pleasure from working hard. I have always worked very long hours. I balance this, though, by taking wonderfully extravagant vacations and spending time with friends and family on weekends.

Choose your aspirations.

It isn't mentally healthy to strive for an impossible goal. It's important to choose your aspirations and be realistic in how you think you can attain them.

CHOOSE YOUR COMMITMENTS

I will:

- ❏ *Declare my goals*
- ❏ *Make hard choices*
- ❏ *Work hard, play hard*
- ❏ *Be realistic about my aspirations*

Notes:

Understand the Trade-Offs

Betsy Cohen
Vice President Extended Enterprise & Futurist
Nestle Purina Petcare Company

Betsy was so kind in returning my email introduction. She said, "Of course I remember you! I've been watching your company and web site with interest!" While we met for the first time nearly four years ago, she's always had an eye on the future.

Work/life balance is a way of life for me.

One reason I went into corporate America and not to an investment bank or consulting firm is that I thought there would be better balance and less travel (not away from home many weeks of the month). This was correct.

Also, I think being in the mid-west has led to a more balanced lifestyle. I experience less commuting time as well as more company and community values supporting the family verses fast-paced cities like Boston, New York, San Francisco, or Los Angeles.

I am married with two teen-age sons and have stayed at one company for many years. Picking a great company like Purina was a key element; I knew I wasn't going to need a lot of moving to other cities to improve my career as I was in a two-career family.

I champion my personal as well as my company's values.

I work for a company that has good work/family values and benefits. I have worked personally to use these benefits and enhance them for others, such as: co-founding the company's childcare center, helping organize summer camp opportunity fairs and mentoring other parents as they balance their work and lives away from work. Being a big fan of quality child care centers where the staff can be babysitters when needed, for example, makes business travel more comfortable for everyone.

Understand that there may be consequences for making Balance choices.

I think work/family balance is important, but when you make this choice, you have to realize that it may change your career opportunities because there are people who can and will give more hours, time and travel than you want to. You have to get comfortable with this idea and say that it is okay for you.

Good companies are working to understand that while people are different, we all add value. For instance, there are some people willing to do crazy work and travel, some who have a more moderate workload, and some who work reduced hours.

Know what you want and let people know.

My advice is to be flexible and know what you are striving for and what you are willing to trade off. If you're willing to travel all week for a limited time on specific projects, let people know that. But if you won't move for a new position, be clear on that as well.

Seek out other women who are a step or two ahead of you on the career or family timeline and get their advice. You may be amazed at the ways they have found to either do more than you think is possible or get comfortable with having to scale back certain portions of their work demands and rewards.

Keep many options open and realize that women who want to have families may have different career paths from those who don't. And if a working woman has a husband who is willing to be the "at home" parent and let the woman be as hard driving as she wants, then quicker career progress can be made. But if the woman is also a key player with home duties plus work responsibilities, the early childhood years will take some patience and understanding. Sanity requires some pacing on all fronts.

Make sure you keep connecting with your family.

I also recommend that you pay attention to your husband and kids. Don't take them for granted. Find ways to connect with each one in special ways.

My older son is now in college. We talk once a week and email sometimes. But more specially, when I travel I now write to him on the hotel stationery so that he gets real paper mail from me. This is making my business trips more fun, and he told me over parents' weekend that in his desk drawer he is saving my letters from "those strange hotels." I take my younger son to school and savor the time with him. I plan really special holidays and family trips to build good memories.

Bonding is so important and fun.

CHOOSE YOUR COMMITMENTS

I will:

☐   *Structure my career to fit my values*
☐   *Work for companies that fit with my values*
☐   *Champion balance initiatives in my company*
☐   *Accept potential trade-offs inherent in my decisions*
☐   *Bond with my family*
☐   *Seek advice from other women*
☐   *Be patient*

Notes:

Take a Long-term View

Linda Goldstein
Partner
Hall Dickler Kent Goldstein & Wood

This is a case where tenacity on both sides paid off! The first time I called Linda's office she was traveling on business. Her admin gave me her cell number; I called and left her a message. She returned my call during a meeting break, only to get my voicemail. We tried to set up a time to talk that evening, but it didn't work out.

Once she returned to her office, she called me but decided she wanted some time to think about the issue so we scheduled a meeting time. When the time came, we had to reschedule due to a conflict. Finally, we connected. Linda was in complete focus and spoke with the amazing intelligence and clarity she is known to possess. It was worth the wait.

I balance over time and manage the imbalance in the moment.

One of the greatest lessons I've learned about the issue of work/life balance is that *balance is a long term goal.* Each day provides us with a measure of imbalance. It is unrealistic to expect that we will incur equal amounts of work and family obligations at any given moment, day, week, and so on. The key is to take a broader perspective on the issue of balance and manage the inevitable imbalance on a day-to-day basis.

Managing the imbalance requires gaining the support from others.

I have never had perfect balance in my life; I have had, however, a virtually perfect support system. My husband is a very supportive husband and thoroughly respectful of my career and goals. As such, we have a true sharing of responsibilities which has helped enormously.

I also have benefited from a very stable home support system that helps ensure everything gets done. And, I have never taken it for granted.

Finally, I have learned to use my work management skills at home, delegating control in managing the household whenever possible.

My children come first. Period.

While my children are the most important priority in my life, I can't always assume that they have the maturity to understand this when I work every day. Therefore, throughout my career I have made it a priority to communicate regularly with them, reinforcing my perspective that they are #1.

I have explained to my children the demands of my job and subsequently they have a healthy respect for what I do. They know, however, that if there is ever a conflict between work and them, they will win. They also know that they can find me whenever they need me. I have a policy that everyone I work with knows: If my children call, I will take the call. This provides my children with a sense of security that they come first and can reach out to me and find me anytime, anywhere.

Providing a sense of devotion to my family is important.

While it may sound clichéd, I make sure that I focus on the quality of time and not the quantity of time that I spend with my family. This requires that I make a clear separation between the time I spend with my family and the time I spend working.

I have found that it is better to leave the house to do my work rather than do work from home. I learned that when I work from home, it sends a mixed message to my children. It says, "I am here for you but being on the phone or the computer is more important." That's why when I am home with my family, I show them that I am completely there for them.

It's a personal, self-imposed choice that my personal needs come last.

While I don't recommend it, I must say that I generally put my personal needs last. But I wouldn't necessarily characterize it that way all the time. My personal need is that my career and my home life are each taken care of properly. That in itself relieves my stress.

Balance is easier when you've established credibility in your career.

Developing a secure and stable career provides professional freedom. This, in turn, provides balance. I worked for many years establishing my reputation and credibility so that today I have the job flexibility to do what I need to do to maintain balance with my family. My colleagues and clients know that I am extremely professional so they don't question my motives or actions if I take time away from the office to attend to other life issues.

I take a long term view on the balance issue.

I have realized that the path to balance is a long continuum and that priorities change over time. My sense of balance has changed continuously based on the stage of my career and the ages of my children. However, overall, I have achieved a healthy and stable balance in my life.

CHOOSE YOUR COMMITMENTS

I will:
- ☐ *Take a long-term view regarding balance*
- ☐ *Accept and manage imbalance*
- ☐ *Develop a support system and delegate tasks*
- ☐ *Put my children first and let everyone, including them, know it in tangible ways*
- ☐ *Be accessible to my kids at all times*
- ☐ *Practice devotion and focus*
- ☐ *Work towards freedom*

Turn Off the Passion

Klaudia Flannigan
Vice President & Account Director
GSD&M

When I told Klaudia what I was working on and asked for her help she exploded in excitement! As it turns out, she's passionate about "work/life balance" and has taken the role of the office champion – circulating articles to and starting discussions with her colleagues.

Balance is downright impossible.

All this talk about "balance" of work and life. So 1996. A few years ago, somebody hit the nail on the head by pointing out that we don't want to sacrifice (balance implies sacrifice on some part).

Not only don't we want to sacrifice anything, it's almost down right impossible for those of us with families, jobs we love, outside interests, inside interests or basically interests in anything we think about, see, or touch.

We are those stereotypical "Type A" personalities. I once read an article about filling up your bucket. "Put the big rocks in first (the important things in your life), then fill in the cracks with the little rocks." All I could think was that *they are all big rocks! There are no little rocks in my life.*

Recently I read an editor's page note entitled "Choose Your Passion." I got what she was saying but as much as she thought she was one of us, she clearly wasn't.

I have passionitis.

Those of us with passionitis can't make simple choices like that. I would argue that passion, itself, has chosen us. Not how we go about life, but who we are at the core of our being. Choosing our passion is too mild a request. Like choosing what's for dinner. Kind of like saying, see 20/20 with your eyes. We have to choose to *turn off the passion* every moment of our lives. Go out and get those eyes fixed. Start a "not to do" list as Jim Collins says in *Good To Great*. Decide moment by moment what is *worthy* of my passion.

The equation becomes [passion in = energy out]. I don't have unlimited energy. I'm human. So what *today*, right now, *deserves* my passion? Is it worth the withdrawal from my energy bank?

Make small changes over time.

It's like being an alcoholic. One day at a time, one moment at a time, one step at a time. No New Year's resolutions or life-altering changes. Start little and end up changed. And I say this not being successful at turning anything off yet.

Choose not to be passionate.

Choose not to be passionate has become a code among me and my passion-aholic friends for when we are over thinking, over worrying, or *over anything* on things that shouldn't matter so much. They don't *deserve* my energy withdrawal. We will now abruptly end those discussions with *"I don't want to think about this anymore, I'm not passionate enough about it."* (That's a good thing).

So good luck to all you passion-aholics out there. Think small. Think: What I am *not* passionate about today?

CHOOSE YOUR COMMITMENTS

I will:
- ☐ *Turn off the passion*
- ☐ *Start a "not to do" list*
- ☐ *Decide what is worthy of my passion*
- ☐ *Take it one day at a time*

Notes:

Rebalance Your Life

Christin DeVries
Director of Promotional Marketing
CBS TV Network

While interviewing Anne O'Grady for this project, she said, "You need to talk to Christin DeVries! She's doing a great job balancing!" I gave her a call and initially she felt she'd been misrepresented. But then she realized that maybe Anne was right.

It hasn't been a big issue.

I have to admit, the whole work/life balance issue has not been a big issue for me. Most of my life outside of work includes people I work with during the day. And, given what I do for a living (TV!), even when I go home and watch TV, I'm working. Good thing I love my job!

My life is now more complicated; we share responsibilities.

I am finding, however, that as I get older and my life gets more complicated the work/life balance issue is more relevant.

A few months ago I had a baby. Before I had him I wouldn't mind what time I came home: now it is important that I have at least one hour with him before he goes to bed. Also, weekends have taken on a new significance of being family time. Having a baby in my life has made me "rebalance" the way I think and what I do regarding work/life balance.

My husband is great. He and I share the home responsibilities very well. For example, I am the morning day care "dropper-offer" and he is the "picker-upper" in the evenings. We each have our feeding schedules for the baby. And one night he'll pick something up for dinner, the next night I'll cook. We constantly juggle back and forth to accommodate travel and work schedules, looking to ease the load on each other.

Take each day as it comes.

I take each day as it comes, focusing on the quality of my time and not the quantity of it. I make the time I have at work or at home with my family the best I can make it.

I know every so often, I'll need to rebalance again.

CHOOSE YOUR COMMITMENTS

I will:
- ❑ *Re-balance my life*
- ❑ *Love my job, or leave it*
- ❑ *Plan time wisely*
- ❑ *Share/delegate home responsibilities*

Notes:

Balance Self

Kim Scheffler
North American Intimate Apparel Business Manager
Invista (formerly Dupont)

Kim's first response to this project was that it was "fabulous!" It was apparent from the beginning of the interview that she had a great deal of energy for the topic.

It's more about self-balance than work/life balance.

Yes, work/life balance is a constant struggle. But, I don't know if the solution is finding the balance between work and life. For me it is more about finding the right balance among work/home/self.

I have two wonderful children and a very supportive husband. But life is not just home. While it is a tremendous responsibility being a wife and mother, I also know it is a tremendous responsibility just being me. I try really hard not to get the short end of the stick in taking care of myself.

For me, balance is a matter of focus.

Last spring I gave some intensive focus to this issue and learned that while many alternate methods can be used to achieve balance, for me it is about focusing on one thing at a time. When I play with Legos®, I play with Legos. When I'm on a conference call, I'm on the call. It is more than about actions, though; it is about trying to separate my brain from the way it works. While my tendency is to integrate these two parts of my being, I have learned that I can't be everything all of the time.

Children changed everything.

Everyone had always told me that having children is a life-changing event. I didn't understand what they were talking about until it happened to me.

For the first time in my life, following the birth of my son, everything else had to stop. And I mean stop. I couldn't go anywhere or do anything else for the first days and weeks following his birth. It was the first time someone else was in complete control over me!

After my child was born, I learned I was out of balance without work in my life!

Ever so gradually, my life became my own again. I could once again be selective about what took up my time. And one thing I wanted back in my life was working outside the home. I learned that I needed it, that I was actually out of balance without it!

Now with two children, I am fortunate that I can afford the best facilities for them. They have my love and support and the support of experts who are teaching them wonderful things on a daily basis. Moreover, they are learning social skills and having fun by interacting with kids their own age. They love it, and so do I. We're all happier as a result.

Being a mom is a full-time job, but I manage it by taking smart shortcuts.

At first I wondered if I was being a good mom; was I giving my children enough of me? Now I know that I am and I don't feel guilty about making smart choices that help!

For example, this year I didn't hand make their Halloween costumes: I purchased them. This weekend I'm taking my kids to a birthday party and signed up to bring the plates and napkins so that I didn't have to take the time to bake. And, I'm okay with it. My kids don't really know the difference: we're achieving the same goals, and my life isn't out of balance as a result.

I learned the hard way.

I'll never forget the first time in my life that I couldn't "do everything." I was a first line supervisor at a manufacturing plant. Prior to this position, I had always prided myself on how I could manage everything. I had managed getting a Chemical Engineering degree from an Ivy League school, maintained a long-term relationship with my boyfriend, and found time to be with friends and family. But managing 32 people on rotating shifts while I was day based was overwhelming. My parents had always taught me that I could do anything. What they forgot to share, however, was that I cannot do *everything*.

That same year my dear grandmother passed away. Sitting at her funeral I looked around at my family and realized something that changed my life. I could be easily replaced at work but I could never be replaced in the lives of the people sitting in that room.

I have the right to balance myself.

The most important thing I have done in achieving work/life balance, though, is giving myself the right to put me in the equation.

Two activities that help me remain personally balanced are exercising and scrapbooking. This is something that I have done for years and I find it incredibly rewarding. It serves many purposes.

Scrapbooking is something I do to connect with friends and family as well as to provide myself with support.

I spend about a Friday night a month with my friends doing this. It reminds me of what quilting bees must have been like. We are all scrapbook enthusiasts, attending three-day/two-night scrapbooking conventions twice a year, but we also have much more in common.

These women are a vital part of my support network. They have insight into what local doctors are the best, what schools and teachers might be right for my children, and other "life" issues that I would have to spend much more time on if it weren't for their guidance and advice.

Scrapbooking also helps connect me with my family. Just last week my son and I worked on a Christmas scrapbook that highlighted him over the past five years. Together, we picked out what pictures of him we wanted to use. He was in charge of finding stickers and other personal elements for the page.

Sometimes I even do scrapbooks on my business trips and for others in my office. For instance, one of my colleagues was battling cancer and we put together a scrapbook that showed how much we cared.

I have to decide what is right for me.

I keep reminding myself that energy and time are finite resources. It's like a pie with only so many slices to go around. The pie never gets any bigger.

I have a daily reminder.

I have a little painting that hangs above my light switch at work so that I remind myself of this fact twice a day. It reads, "Never get so busy making a living that you forget to make a life."

CHOOSE YOUR COMMITMENTS

I will:

- ❑ *Find self balance*
- ❑ *Focus on one thing at a time*
- ❑ *Stop being everything to everybody*
- ❑ *Decide what I want in my life*
- ❑ *Let others help*
- ❑ *Take smart shortcuts*
- ❑ *Do things for me*

Be a Live-a-holic

Nancy Crozier
National Branding Advisor
The Nature Conservancy

Nancy is one of the most vibrant and joyous women you'll ever meet. She's been in marketing for more than 30 years. We met during our time together at the American Red Cross some fifteen years ago. With a creative philosopher's soul, she brings a level of depth and perspective rare in today's rational world.

As a creative marketer, I have never been off duty.

I cannot remember a time when I didn't work – or a time when I didn't have a high-level leadership role in either the non-profit or for-profit sectors. I love work; it is my passion – my life.

I found that I was always juicing, and not being juiced.

I thought I was having a heart-attack, but I am grateful it was only acid reflux. The stress and pressure of managing more than a hundred staff had finally caught up with me and started causing health problems. I had to let go in order to achieve joy.

The desert called my name.

Having spent most of my life in Washington DC, I needed the nourishment that only the desert could provide. I proposed a new position to the Conservancy (the largest environmental organization in the world) that would allow me to work from home in the beauty of the desert hills. They said, "yes"! My husband, a senior executive as well, also found a new position that allowed us to move to Scottsdale a couple of months ago.

Having said this, I don't think balance is the right issue.

For me, I think of work as taking a creative field trip. There is often no distinction between my work and life because the experiences and energy in my life feed my work and vice versa. The work itself is so replenishing that it provides balance in itself.

Most of the successful women that I know thrive on productivity and view any down time that they may have as the time when *productivity comes to them.* The creative stimulation of passionate engagement with life is the way they become refueled. And refueled as a whole person.

If the balance issue exists at all, it is the balance each woman finds among her mind, body, soul, and spirit.

Unless you look closely, the work-a-holic and the live-a-holic can seem similar. They are driven, assertive, and successful. But the work-a-holics are toxic. They are one-dimensional. They have no balance, no glow about them, no joy. They are stale and draw your energy from you. The liva-holic is different. She lives her life to the fullest, produces at high levels, and provides energy to others. She embarks on projects and has no idea of the time as it passes by. This comes from possessing *equal amounts of joy and intensity.*

I have a personal formula I check in on every day.

Every day I keep track of my amounts of joy and intensity. My formula breaks down into the areas of mind, body, soul, and spirit. And when I see one of these areas not being refueled, I take *purposefully unorthodox actions* to get me back on track. For instance, if my mind is out of balance, I might uncharacteristically watch a television program on quantum mechanics to stimulate me.

The key is to find work that is replenishing in itself.

With the sun setting over the desert sky, how can I not feel replenished as I look out my home office window? Nature itself replenishes the soul.

CHOOSE YOUR COMMITMENTS

I will:

- ❑ *Be a live-a-holic, not a work-a-holic*
- ❑ *Create a role that works for me*
- ❑ *Nurture my mind, body, spirit, and soul*

Live in the Now

Marcy Cona
Creative Director / Director of Education
Clairol
Procter & Gamble

It was a miracle that I got through to Marcy; the working mother of three was on one of her twice-monthly business trips to New York City. I heard her excuse herself from a meeting to take my call.

I live in the now.

My navigation skills among work, children, wife, mother, and life, rest on one idea: Living in the now.

I used to operate on the "get through" theory. You know, "get through the task, get through the day, get through the week." One day I realized that I was just getting through life. I had to accept the fact that I don't have any form of balance in the traditional sense.

I accepted balance on my own terms.

I accepted the idea of "balance" on my terms: It is a moving target. With this perspective I am no longer frustrated with my inability to achieve the traditional version of balance. Now I'm happy.

As one of six children with two hard-working parents, I was taught to focus on what "could be." They instilled in me a zest for life that I am grateful for. However, that zest can suddenly inundate my life.

I used to think managing my zestful life was about making lists and feeling a sense of accomplishment through completion. I now realize that it is more about living my zestful life by understanding the relationships among the highs, lows and midpoints.

Mom, you need to relax.

Let me share a low point with you. Last week I was on another business trip and it was a disaster. I forgot my computer cord, my cell phone, and if that wasn't enough, I lost my wallet! Luckily a man found my wallet and went to great lengths to find me (he found my hotel frequency card in the wallet and went about checking to see if I was there!). When I returned home my seven-year-old son said, "Mom, you need to relax a little." He was right.

I focus on the now and don't feel guilty about putting me first.

At first I struggled with work/life balance because I set myself up for failure. I was everything to everyone. I was always thinking about the past and the future, allowing those thoughts to interrupt my concentration and I went out of control.

Now I've set up boundaries and am protective of myself and those around me. I focus on the "now," enjoying the moments at the moment they occur and not worrying about yesterday and tomorrow.

Finally, I don't feel guilty saying it's about "me first." Before, I would say "yes" to just about anyone who needed anything – at work or at home. I've learned to sincerely smile and simply say "no." I don't feel the need to explain, find excuses, or feel guilty. If I am happy, everyone is happy. And now I am happy.

CHOOSE YOUR COMMITMENTS

I will:
- ❑ *Live in the now*
- ❑ *Accept balance on my own terms*
- ❑ *Relax*
- ❑ *Stop being everything to everybody*
- ❑ *Set up boundaries*
- ❑ *Put "me" first*
- ❑ *Just say " no" and smile*

Notes:

Build a Support Network

Tena Barnes
Marketing Director
Rhodes Furniture

Tena returned my call, as she often does, on her cell phone during her long after-work drive home in Atlanta traffic.

The balance issue is constantly evolving.

My family and close friends are extremely important to me but I also love the career path I'm on and the work that I do. Balancing family/work/life is a constant juggling act that for me is constantly evolving.

I have a strong support network.

I have found two areas that help me maintain a balance. I have a strong support network of family and friends as well as business and social organizations. We all help each other out depending on the need, which alleviates a lot of day-in and day-out pressures.

I make sure to have time for myself.

I also think it's important to make time for myself. My husband and I have a pact. We each have small blocks of time scheduled on a weekly basis that is considered "my time." I can spend that time doing anything I want for me - taking a long walk, going out with friends, reading a book, or just relaxing in a chair with a glass of wine!

CHOOSE YOUR COMMITMENTS

I will:

☐ **Build a support network**

☐ **Make time for myself**

Notes:

Adjust & Overcome

Lisa Gavales
Senior Vice President of Marketing Strategy
Bloomingdale's

Like one of my high school girlfriends, Lisa drew me in and made me feel like a trusted confidant. Sharp as a tack, it's apparent that she knows how to use her talents and skills to opt-in to the life she desires.

Balance became exponentially more difficult after having my daughter four years ago.

I had wanted to have a child for a long time. The year I became pregnant with my daughter I was on business travel a total of twenty-six weeks (amazing I became pregnant at all given that schedule!). After I learned that I was pregnant, I knew I had some decisions to make.

Together, my boss and I assessed the situation.

As a retail General Merchandising Manager (GMM), I held a position on the Executive Committee. With that role comes a tremendous amount of responsibility and travel. While I loved the job and had been very successful in my career, looking forward I knew that if I kept up that pace I wouldn't have a chance to get to know my daughter.

I'm not sure I buy into the notion that women are *choosing not to be at the top*, that they opt-out. What I do know is that for the time being I chose balance.

So when this position opened up, I took the lateral move in part because it offered me a lifestyle that fits with being a mom. While I still work long hours, at least my travel schedule is manageable, allowing me time with my daughter.

There is no "off" switch.

Traveling with another executive last week, we noticed that we were both more tired and not having as much fun as we used to have. We realized that there has become less and less time for us to decompress. There's no off switch. All the time we have is spent on someone else's issues.

I'm so busy I don't need keys.

I lost my keys for three months and didn't even notice. I leave the house in the morning and the nanny is there, so I don't have to lock the door behind me. In order to save two hours each day commuting to the city, I live two walking blocks from work, so I don't need car keys. I arrive at work and the doors are always open. I go home, and my husband is there already so I can walk right in. My life is so occupied by others that I don't even need a key.

But it's not forever.

In business, we manage the day-to-day with an eye on the longer term. That's how I think about my work/life balance. Today, I am doing what needs to be done in order to live the life I want. As my life changes, I'm keeping my options open for the longer term.

CHOOSE YOUR COMMITMENTS

I will:

- ☐ *Discuss potential alternative positions with my company*
- ☐ *Decompress!*
- ☐ *Keep everything in perspective, remembering that it's never forever*

Notes:

Speak Up

Kim Kulick
Manager of Advertising, Interactive & Public Relations
BP

At first, Kim wasn't sure that I wanted to hear about the work/life balance issues among single working women, as it is often spoken about as a "women with children" issue. Clearly, the work/life balance issue is broader than that and single women everywhere can thank Kim for her ability to speak up and articulate the needs of all women.

Work chose me.

For some reason, people don't expect that single women executives want work/life balance. I have had it said to me, "You chose work." They have it backwards, "Work chose me."

While it's true that I don't have a child to take care of at home, I still have a life. I have family and friends and goals and aspirations that exist beyond the walls of my work environment.

Like many women, earlier in my career I felt the need to prove myself by working long hours and always putting work ahead of everything else. After years of establishing my credibility and performance as an employee, I don't feel guilty about leaving early. I'm confident that I'm an effective, dedicated employee and don't need to stay late to prove it.

Time doesn't equal commitment.

When I accepted my current position I made it very clear with my new boss that I no longer feel guilty making the decision to allow myself to leave work by 5:30 p.m. on most nights. I would take anyone to the mat that doesn't think I am committed and dedicated to my work. It just so happens that I am committed and dedicated to my life as well. And, I received no resistance from my manager, only support.

It's a personal issue.

Work/life balance is a personal issue – it affects everyone. As such, I believe that it should be treated the same way for everyone.

Maintain standards while allowing flexibility.

The bottom line is that the work needs to get done, and done well. My expectations are high and everyone knows it. So, I am not flexible on that issue. Where I am flexible is where and how the work gets done.

As a manager, I am sensitive to those who report to me. I am very supportive of setting up flextime work schedules for those who need to come in early and leave early or vice versa due to personal home situations. I also try not to set up late meetings which make people uncomfortable when they need to leave early.

Speak up to management.

In addition to adjusting my own management style, I have supported the issue with leadership and human resources. Only by sharing our perspectives with policy makers can we make a big difference.

In many companies I believe that people like to talk about what they do to support work/life balance, but in many cases it doesn't *feel* like they support it. It is almost an unwritten rule that we keep it a secret that some employees work from home or have flex-time. It is thought of this way - if others found out that it was allowed more people would want to do it, some of whom wouldn't be able to manage themselves away from the office environment to the same level of productivity. And, while some may not, it does us no harm to implement assessment tools for those who would like to try.

We shouldn't accommodate balance; we should accept it.

Even the way we talk about how we address work/life balance issues needs to be changed. We talk about accommodating women who have work/life balance needs. To me it is just real life. So we shouldn't "accommodate" it, but rather accept and embrace it.

Employees cannot be productive and successful if they are worried about what is going on at home or that they'll be fired if they need to stay home with a sick child.

People ultimately run companies. And, only by treating them as individuals and understanding their goals, work ethic, and personal needs can corporations retain the best and brightest.

CHOOSE YOUR COMMITMENTS

I will:

- ☐ *Speak up*
- ☐ *Support all women*
- ☐ *Stop trying to prove myself*
- ☐ *Maintain my standards*
- ☐ *Adjust my management style*
- ☐ *Accept work/life balance as a real issue*

Notes:

__Settle In With Your Work Family__

Anne Murray
Director of Integrated Marketing
Southwest Airlines

I sent Anne an email and within hours her administrative assistant called to set up an interview time. I would have to wait three days to hear what she had to say, but it was worth the wait. Many times impatience gets the best of me, but Anne knows better.

Can we ever really feel 100% satisfied?

How do we think we'll ever be in a position to say that we're 100% perfect at what boils down to a relationship issue? Even if we did achieve balance in between our relationships at work and at home, we wouldn't know it. When it comes to matters such as these we're always striving to be better.

I achieve balance by doing whatever I can to strengthen my relationships at home, with my friends and family, and with my *work family.*

Like a family, Southwest Airlines understands the ebbs and flows in my life.

My company knows me – I've been with them a long time. And just like my family, they know I have my good times and bad. They know that I always come through in the end and that I'll always be there for the critical moments.

My struggle with work/life balance issues has ebbed and flowed over the years and they cut me some slack when I need it. I've also built a terrific team that I know I can count on to help.

In turn, I have compassion for others.

I have a manager reporting to me who has a six month old baby. And while she is performing exceptionally well and is happy working, I can feel her struggles and guilt. It brings back the emotion I felt as a new working mother.

When my daughter was young she was in Brownies. They have a "flying up" ceremony when they graduate to Girl Scouts, some time in the 2nd grade. I was on a business trip and couldn't attend so my husband (of now 23 years) went alone. Afterwards, he said that it really was a "mom thing" as he was the only dad there. While I know it opened my daughter's mind to alternative roles for men *and* women (which is a good thing), I couldn't help but feel that all to common pang of guilt and regret that I wasn't there for her. Now, you might say that in the grand scheme of things a "flying up" ceremony isn't a critical life-altering event. But, here it is more than ten years later and I feel it like it was just yesterday.

Turning back to my new mother manager, it is my turn to make sure that she has every opportunity to manager her work/life balance successfully.

The humanness of my company is inspiring.

I've been at Southwest Airlines since my oldest, now 20-years old, was in kindergarten. When you work here, it is so much more than work; it is a way of life. It is 24/7, but in the best possible way. It really becomes a second family. Southwest Airlines and the people I work with *are* my support system – and that has made all the difference.

Just like a family, we rally around each other and provide whatever is needed at the time. For example, this past year I received a telephone call from a hospital in New York to come as quickly as possible; my mother had taken a turn for the worse and had only a few days to live. My boss said, "Just go and do what you need to do, we'll handle everything here."

By the time my plane arrived in New York, the hospital had begun receiving an overflow of cards, letters, and flowers from my *work family*. I didn't even know it was possible, but somehow they even had food delivered during the days I was there. The funeral was a few days later and two members of my *Southwest Airlines family* flew to New York to be by my side. The humanness of this company is beyond belief.

<u>CHOOSE YOUR COMMITMENTS</u>
I will:
- ❏ *Build a stable career with one company*
- ❏ *Choose a compassionate company*
- ❏ *Be compassionate with my employees*

<u>*Develop Others*</u>

Rebeca Johnson
Vice President of Marketing
Frito-Lay North America

Becky was so passionate about this topic that she called me from home during some needed time off to take care of a family issue. Her perspective and insight on the work/life balance issue is particularly relevant given her current situation.

The idea of Balance is a myth.

The work/life balance issue is often compared to a scale, in which one side inevitably evens out the other side at some point in time. Executive women have chosen a heavy load and to perpetuate image of some steady state of balance is unrealistic. The whole notion of balance is not achievable.

Balance is dynamic, not static.

Unlike the static image of a scale, I feel achieving balance is more analogous to a sailboat on the water. When sailing, I find myself moving with the wind, constantly adjusting the sails to let the wind help carry me along. I work with the changing winds instead of fighting them. Sometimes I'm moving in one direction, sometimes in another. But I always end up where I want to be.

The changing corporate environment requires stamina.

I remember the days when in corporations we had cycles of time when we worked nonstop. These days, however, we are always revving as business challenges, presentations, and so forth keep coming at us. There is no such thing as down time.

The way I tackle the stamina required for balance is ensuring I have the depth and breadth of a solid team under me.

Today, more that ever, it is critical to develop a team of professionals to rely on to fill in the gaps. I spend a lot of time on recruitment, ensuring that I hire only the best. I then invest in their training and development to make sure that they can step in when someone on the team, myself included, needs time to balance out personal issues.

For example, last Friday night my husband was admitted to the hospital with chest pains and they found a blockage. Thankfully, he is going to be fine, but I left the office immediately and took today [Monday] off and am planning on not going back to work until this Thursday so that I can be there for him.

The needs of the business continue regardless of my personal issues. Our 2004 plans are due and we have to bring in the year. My team is back at the office handling these things for me for the time being. Additionally, today I was supposed to be in New York City for a meeting with Viacom. One of my direct reports stepped up and is handling it. She has my cell phone number in case she has questions or needs input on a decision. I have complete confidence in my team to carry the load until I return.

Development in your team pays off in a huge way – I am living proof.

Frito-Lay is a part of my family's life.

I have three incredibly wonderful children, ages 16, 8 and 8 (twins!). They have never had the perspective that mom goes off to work and disappears and then reappears some time later. From the beginning I have made what I do visible to them and natural for them.

I have integrated my family and my work. I am very flexible about how my work gets done. Getting the work done between 8:00 a.m. and 6:00p.m. on weekdays and not working weekends just isn't realistic.

Sometimes I'll sit at the kitchen table at 10:00 p.m. or pick up emails from home on Sunday mornings. I even pull emails off my palm pilot during soccer practice!

From the time my children were born they have come into work with me. By the time my oldest was in 2nd grade she could write marketing decks! I've even taken my children on business trips with me. They understand that many of the things we enjoy as a family are a result of what I do at work. Bringing them to work allows them to understand for themselves that that means.

I am very clear about my priorities.

When you have a family emergency as I did last week, it provides you with the opportunity to reflect on your priorities and decisions. Once again, I reinforced the fact that my priority is my family as I just walked away from work when they needed me. When I reflect on my decisions regarding work/life balance over the years, I have to admit that I wouldn't do anything differently.

CHOOSE YOUR COMMITMENTS

I will:

☐ *Develop a strong team and trust them to perform*

☐ *Fill in for women who need me*

☐ *Integrate work and life*

☐ *Let my children see first hand what I do*

☐ *Put family first*

Notes:

Remember Your Values

Marcia Hanford
Director of National Promotions
BVHE - Disney

I had a hard time literally finding Marcia! Evidently, she's changed buildings and phone numbers twice since I last spoke with her which was easily a year ago. I sent her an email hoping she would reply. A day later, at 11:16 p.m., she sent the email which you see below.

Unfortunately, I don't have any quotes for you right now.

Other than this: My life is the picture in the dictionary of "no balance." For nearly two years, my life has been out of balance, and my focus is on getting it back where it should be.

I have never been one to place my job above my personal life, but that is what has occurred as the result of this economy and the downsizing and enormous workloads placed upon us remaining workers.

I'm considering a realignment of my life.

I constantly evaluate the stress of being unemployed verses the stress of this situation. I trust that fate will lead me to the correct destination. I am seriously contemplating resigning and enjoying the freedom and risk of consulting work. While eventually that is where I want to be, it's not quite on my plan due to terrible practical matters of medical coverage and such benefits.

I know better; it's just my turn to suffer.

My consolation is: I do know better. I am not fooled. I just think it is our generation's time to suffer through adversity, much as earlier generations suffered through depressions and wars. This is our time. The basic values are there—but enough roses aren't being smelled.

I do not consider myself a successful corporate executive.

I'm a middle management type who has enjoyed the opportunities and experiences of this career, but in no way would it have been worth sacrificing time with family and friends *if that choice had ever come to me.*

As it is, I am single so unfortunately too many hours are at the office not because I don't have anything else to do but because I'm so darn conscientious. I'm working daily on becoming more selfish and developing a thicker skin toward unfinished work.

I'm hitting the "send" button without even proofreading. This just came out of my fingertips.

<u>CHOOSE YOUR COMMITMENTS</u>

I will:

- ☐ *Evaluate my career options*
- ☐ *Understand this is a short term condition*
- ☐ *Have a sense of humor*
- ☐ *Stop being so darn conscientious*
- ☐ *Be more selfish*
- ☐ *Develop thicker skin*

Notes:

Don't Do "Should Do's"

Cathy Dowdell
Sr. Research Services Manager, New Products
SC Johnson... A Family Company

Cathy was out of breath when she picked up the telephone. Right off the bat she wanted to participate but needed to do it on her own time. So, all it took was my email address and a few days later her email hit my desk.

Commit to your passions.

Between work/life and community service, I don't know that I'm managing them all that well especially since I got a new assignment in July.

What works best for me is only committing to the things I'm really passionate about. So I say "yes" at work to extra assignments that truly interest me and try, whenever possible, to say "no" to those that don't.

I raise money for my undergraduate alma mater, but don't help with other types of projects. I focus my relationship time on my husband, parents, sisters and just a couple good friends, and just don't find much time for acquaintances.

Deal with things immediately and move on.

One incredibly simple idea that has made a real impact on my time is something I used to be horrible about -

- paper! A piece of paper has only one purpose, and that is to be dealt with immediately. And there are only three options - put it where it belongs immediately, put things I really want to read in a "read later" pile (one at work and one at home), or throw it away. If it's not important enough to fit in the first two, then it belongs in the third.

Stop doing "should do's" and focus on what's important.

To me, balance is a feeling - a sense of being. Balance means never making decisions based on "should," but on things that are important to me as well as those close to me. Balance means time to myself to refuel as well as sharing my time in community service.

CHOOSE YOUR COMMITMENTS

I will:
- ❑ ***Commit to my passions***
- ❑ ***Focus my time***
- ❑ ***Stop doing "Should Do's"***
- ❑ ***Deal with things immediately and move on***

Notes:

Create the Life You Want

Bronwyn Morgan
Sr. Manager, Entertainment & Strategic Alliances
The Coca-Cola Company

Bronwyn had been out of the office for a few days on business and although work had piled up on her desk, she took a few minutes to be interviewed for this project. Hers is a powerful message.

I am on a daily journey to get the balance I deserve and desire.

It is critical to me that I take a holistic approach to my life. To do this, I have spent a lot of time reflecting on *who I am and what I want.* Every day I keep in mind *the all of who I am* so that I can be true to myself.

Enjoy every moment of your life.

I treasure every moment of my life, especially focusing on the now. It's all I have! Tomorrow may not show up and, guess what, the past is over.

So, I always take time for me: body, mind and spirit. I also try not to take myself too seriously and put my career in perspective.

Without a "whole" you, nothing else matters.

It is important to me to surround myself with people who lift me up. I have learned that when I help other women in achieving balance for themselves, I find it easier to achieve balance for myself.

Only you have the power to create the life you want.

Never skimp on you. If you don't like the life you have, create a new one! Only you have that power.

CHOOSE YOUR COMMITMENTS

I will:
- ☐ *Know the "whole" of me and what I want*
- ☐ *Work on my mind, body and soul*
- ☐ *Put my career in perspective*
- ☐ *Surround myself with people who lift me up*

Notes:

Focus on What Makes You Happy

Stephanie Provost
Associate Customer Marketing Manager, Skin Category
Unilever HPC

I left Stephanie a voicemail about this project and asked for her help. When she responded, she apologized for being "absolutely nuts." So, while clearing out her email over the weekend, she took some time send a response.

I don't manage balance well.

Many times, I feel like I don't manage a very good balance between life and work. The good thing is that I am single with no children so I am only responsible for myself.

Stay in touch with what's important.

Since my 12-15 hour days tend to burn me out at times, I work out in the morning and try to make dinner plans when my schedule is not as hectic. This keeps me motivated and in touch with what is truly important in my life.

I'm saving "balance" for when my live changes.

Balance is important but I also think it should be saved for when other people's lives that could be affected.

For now, I don't feel guilty working late and being single focused. I guarantee that will change once my life changes.

Focus on things that make you happy.

Choose activities that make you happy, not things that you feel you should do. Stayed focused and only compromise when there is a critical reason to.

CHOOSE YOUR COMMITMENTS

I will:
- ☐ ***Take advantage of non-hectic time***
- ☐ ***Choose activities that make me happy***
- ☐ ***Stop compromising***

Notes:

Learn to Multi-Task

Nancy Barker
Executive Director, Client Management
Cerner Healthcare

Nancy was happy to provide me with input on work/life balance as long as I worked the interview into her exercise schedule. So, I put on my sweats and met up with her during her early morning walk.

I fulfill my personal needs throughout the day.

The key to achieving a work/life balance is effectively multi-tasking. I feel that in order to be at my optimal performance at work, I need to take care of myself first. In order to accommodate my needs, I integrate them throughout the day.

For example, I'll participate in conference calls while I am taking care of other matters. I also believe that keeping healthy by exercising makes me a better and more productive associate. Therefore, instead of taking a standard lunch, I do some form of exercise during the workday. Oftentimes, then, I'll do emails or additional work late at night after my twin five-year olds go to bed.

Multi-tasking is key.

So, for me, the ability to multi-task and flow between meeting personal and work responsibilities helps me achieve balance.

CHOOSE YOUR COMMITMENTS

I will:

- ☐ *Integrate whenever possible my personal and work needs throughout the day*
- ☐ *Exercise everyday*
- ☐ *Master multi-tasking*

Notes:

Make Hard Choices

Andrea Simkins
Senior Director
Corporate Executive Board

It took a few reschedules on both of our parts, but during our interview it became clear that she is confident and focused in her choices.

I feel an immense amount of responsibility at work.

I have always been trained that career success comes from providing tangible deliverables. I have made the personal choice to make sure that my projects are well done and if that means working long hours, so be it.

Senior Management knows they can count on me.

After years of delivering results, my management has rewarded me with a great salary, a talented staff, and increasing responsibility. This has come as a result of my work ethic and dedication to my job. I am proud of what I've been able to achieve.

If I don't deliver, someone else will.

The environment during the past few years has been extremely competitive, especially given the downturn in the economy. With all of the corporate downsizings, there is more competition for good positions which places more pressure on me live up to my leadership's expectations.

My company supports work/life balance.

I have to admit that my company is supports work/life balance issues, however it is difficult for me to be able to achieve this ideal. I have made the decision, though, to focus on work.

I can't have two extraordinary competing priorities in my life right now.

This is an extraordinarily busy time at work and I am under a great deal of pressure. I cannot focus on anything else at the moment, not even my wedding. I have postponed it until 2005 because the next four or five months will need to be totally dedicated to work. Planning a wedding is a huge job and I just don't have the time right now. By postponing the wedding, I have significantly reduced my stress. For now, I am choosing to revolve my personal life around work in order to be truly successful at what I'm doing.

<u>CHOOSE YOUR COMMITMENTS</u>

I will:
- ❑ **Maintain my standing at work**
- ❑ **Make hard choices**

Keep a List

Mimi Dixon
Promotion Manager
Campbell Soup Company

When I called Campbell Soup I was actually looking for Lisa Cuppett. However, her voicemail picked up and stated that she was maternity leave until January and to forward calls to Mimi. When I explained to Mimi what I was calling about, she laughed and said, "I'm handling two jobs right now and I don't have much balance!"

I keep lists.

I focus on the "how" part of achieving a good work/life balance. For me, it is a must have, not a goal that I work towards. So, I manage it like I manage a lot of things. I keep lists.

I believe that women are, by nature, multi-tasking individuals; we like having a lot of things going on. So, I keep a checklist of everything that I need to get done every week.

This list includes all of my corporate responsibilities as well as things that I do for me and others. I make sure that I include at least item "for me" on the checklist each week such as going to the gym, shopping, seeing friends and so forth. I also ensure that I do one thing to help others like helping out a friend or seeing my mother.

I evaluate my performance.

At the end of each week I evaluate *my balance performance*. First, I make sure that I can check of at least 80%-90% of the list – including the items around doing something for me as well as doing things for others. I find that overall I manage it quite well, although there are some seasons [at work] that make it more difficult.

Being in balance means being in control.

Being in balance is really about who I am. If I am off-balance, everything is off kilter. My job becomes more difficult and things around the house just don't get done. So, being in-balance means that I am more in control and ultimately more positive about myself.

CHOOSE YOUR COMMITMENTS

I will:
- ❏ *Keep lists and evaluate my performance*
- ❏ *Do something for me, and for others*

Notes:

Be a Master Planner

Joy Corneliussen
Director of Marketing
Kmart

Joy's name gives you a clue to her personality. Rooted in reality, Joy immediately connected with the topic and used her organizational skills to bring definition to the problem at hand.

I tackle balance through analysis and discipline.

Using the discipline and organizational skills acquired during my career has helped me both at work and at home. Balance is certainly an issue especially when work or family throws you into utter chaos.

Everyone is faced with incremental responsibilities.

Given the economy and downsizing, most companies have to do more with less. Personally, I am wearing more hats than ever and being expected to handle more responsibilities. I know I'm not alone. And, that means more juggling – it doesn't matter who you are.

I find a few quite moments each day to reduce my stress.

Every day I get up before my children to enjoy a few peaceful moments *alone*. I may exercise on my treadmill or simply spend some time thinking and reflecting. While I don't take that long, it is *my personal time* which helps me reduce my stress.

For me, work is how I achieve balance.

While some women opt-out of the corporate life once they have families, for me I achieve balance from work! I know how crazy that must sound, but it is true.

I feel fulfilled by working with people who have common interests such as enjoying solving intellectual challenges and business problems. They also provide me with a network to explore interests outside the work environment.

Make no mistake -- home is where my heart is.

I have a wonderful tag-team husband to our three tween-age daughters. When we are home, we are 100% home. This allows us to experience being a family full time.

At home we plan, plan, and plan.

I have three daughters, and, for instance, when it is swim season, or when one is sick, managing the day-to-day can become insane. So, we make a plan.

Each week we sit down as a family and discuss what activities each of us have planned for the following week. From swim practice and school plays to travel and late meetings, we get it out in the open. We walk through who needs to go where and when, what each of us will be doing, and map out the logistics of how to get it all done.

Getting organized helps us keep the chaos to a minimum and stress levels low.

CHOOSE YOUR COMMITMENTS

I will:

- ❑ **Conduct family planning meetings**
- ❑ **Schedule "alone" time for reflection**
- ❑ **Enact a paradigm shift and choose to think of work as providing me with balance**

Notes:

Focus on What's Important

Claire Rosensweig
President & CEO
Promotion Marketing Association

When Claire answered the telephone I could hear the other line ringing in the background. She said, "Wouldn't you know it, no calls for an hour and now they're backing up! Sorry, go ahead – they'll have to wait."

Focus on work at work, and then leave it there.

It's all about focus. At the end of the day I try to leave work at work. That means that I usually work longer hours during the week.

But, I do carve out "life" time - my time. For instance, weekends are devoted to family, friends, and my significant other.

Know what is important and respect it.

Speaking of my significant other, he and I are both professionals and we understand the importance work plays in our lives and respect what the other is doing.

CHOOSE YOUR COMMITMENTS

I will:
- ❑ *Focus on what's important - carve out "life" time*
- ❑ *Respect my needs and ensure others do too*

__Align Priorities with Behaviors__

Ruth Frantz
Ex-Marketing Director
Clairol

I called Ruth's office only to hear a message indicated that all Clairol business should be directed to another woman and provided another number where Ruth could be reached personally. I dialed. She answered and said, "Oh, boy, do I have a story for you!"

I was a workaholic.

During my years at Clairol, I was a workaholic. Ten or twelve hour days didn't faze me. But then last May, I adopted a little baby girl and my life changed.

While I was among the few retained by Procter & Gamble following their buy-out of Clairol, I decided to step back and reevaluate my life. I made the decision that uprooting my family, moving to Cincinnati, and staying on the fast-paced grind wasn't the right thing to do.

I decided to step back. I left Clairol on very good terms and gave myself some time to breathe.

I am recreating my life.

One of the best things I've done is to hire a Personal Executive Coach. Working with her, I am in the midst of recreating my life so that it works for my daughter, my husband, and me. I took an inventory of my behavior and found that some of the imbalance I was feeling was of my own doing. I wasn't creating boundaries and protecting them.

One of the greatest insights I've uncovered during my six-month journey of self-discovery is that we have the power within ourselves to determine how we live. Looking back, I know that many of the demands I dealt with as a working woman I placed on myself.

I know my priorities.

Now, I am setting my priorities and beginning the search for positions that fulfill my needs. I am re-entering the workforce with a new and different behavior. And, it all started with knowing my priorities.

CHOOSE YOUR COMMITMENTS

I will:
- ❏ *Reevaluate my life – align work/life needs*
- ❏ *Take a self-inventory and set priorities*
- ❏ *Stop placing unnecessary demands on myself*
- ❏ *Set boundaries and protect them*

Notes:

Keep Moving

Anne O'Grady
Senior Vice President of Marketing and Events
CBS Television Network

When I caught up with Anne, her first reaction was to point to people in her company who she thinks are great models for achieving work/life balance. She's like that – shining the light on others. After some coaxing, she talked a little about herself.

My home life is simple now.

Now that my children are grown, achieving balance in my life is easy. My home life is very simple; I don't even own a pet! When I'm faced with a life and work balance issue now, I generally put work first – it is a priority for me.

When it was complicated, I learned to keep moving.

When my children were younger, though, I learned to just keep moving. It was hard in those days and my life wasn't balanced.

I made choices on a daily basis.

I dealt with it by prioritizing and making choices on a daily basis. For instance, this meeting or the school play? While my choice, obviously, was the school play, I did whatever needed to be done. Unfortunately, some times I had to make difficult decisions.

CHOOSE YOUR COMMITMENTS

I will:

- ☐ **Keep moving**
- ☐ **Know my priorities**
- ☐ **Make difficult choices**

Notes:

Plan Balance Strategically

Lisa McCarthy
Executive Vice President
Viacom Plus

It was 7:14 p.m. and I had mere hours until I hit the publishing deadline. Three different interview appointments during the past two days had been made, changed, and finally cancelled due to conflict issues. On a whim I picked up the telephone and called her line to see if she might be available. Her admin answered, "Rhonda! I can't believe it's you! We were going to call but thought we had missed the deadline!" Of course, they had, but I was holding out hope to include her, a known force in empowering women. The first thing she said was, "Tomorrow is Halloween and I want to be with my kids, so I'm working late tonight." This is one Executive Corporate Woman who knows her priorities.

Today's world is busier than ever with more opportunities than ever.

Maintaining and nurturing the many demands in my life is an art. I have many interests: a demanding job, a husband, two children and a huge social circle. I have found that taking a holistic approach works for me. As I age (and, by the way I'm still young), I continue to hone my key focuses and priorities in my life.

I step off the treadmill and take a strategic approach.

When I think about everything I have to do it could be incredibly overwhelming. Rather than taking it as it comes, I step off the treadmill and take a strategic approach.

I look at six months ahead of me and start breaking it down. What needs to be done in the next three months? This week? Today?

I know I can never get it all done, so I don't even try.

I am a big fan of the saying, "You can't have it all but you can have a lot." Everything comes down to your approach to how you handle things. Keeping things in perspective and having the right attitude can make all the difference.

Delegate! Delegate! Delegate!

I'm getting better every year at delegating to others, including my assistant, direct reports, and nanny. They are critical components in making sure that everything is taken care of properly.

Do whatever you can to help others.

Women empowering women is a powerful idea. At Viacom, I started the "Viacom Women's Networking Group" to ensure that executive women across our company have a forum to network and create new possibilities. I believe that there is something each of us can do to help empower other women.

CHOOSE YOUR COMMITMENTS

I will:

- ❑ *Step off the treadmill and think strategically*
- ❑ *Maintain and nurture all of my interests*
- ❑ *Not try to do it all*
- ❑ *Delegate!*

Notes:

Step 3:
Plan for Joy

Plan for Joy & Balance

My only advice is to stay aware, listen carefully,
and yell for help if you need it.
- Judy Bloom

I turned to a trusted colleague and friend of many years to help me with this section of the book.

What follows is the work of Karen Brethower, Ph.D., President of Executive Consultation LLC.

Karen is a leadership and organization consultant who has worked with executives of Fortune 500 companies for more than fifteen years. She specializes in coaching senior executives, talent management, and the planning and facilitation of senior meetings. Each year more women are Plan for Joy and Achieving Balance included in her roster of clients, as more women become senior executives. Find out more about her and contact her by going to www.rtmj.com and clicking on the *Seeking Joy* tab.

I have formatted her work for consistency with the rest of the book and she has included RTM&J® thoughts, particularly regarding Think-Feel-Do (TFD) in her plans.

Why tackle the work/life balance right now?

Each woman executive arrives at a decision to wrestle her calendar to the mat to create her own personal version of balance in a variety of ways.

The three most common occasions to start this 'balancing' work are:

- A calamity – work or personal
- A health crisis – her own or that of someone close
- A sense of never being caught up, of being drained

Since you are reading this book, you may be looking at this issue in advance of a crisis. However, most women are *delivered* to the point of earnestly attempting balance for the first time by one of the sets of circumstances listed above.

As a coach to senior executive women for more than fifteen years, it's become clear that work/life balance usually focuses on the *work* side. For many, executive coaching starts in order to improve performance at work, even when life issues are the immediate focus.

The exceptions are women who are seriously questioning whether they are paying too high a *life* price for their *work* success. Typically, these women do not even mention joy.

That is, they are rarely seeking work/life balance for its own sake. *They don't have time to work on something that conceptual.*

It usually requires some triggering event to perceive the lack of balance and a sense of urgency to change it. Some want to be able to get more done at work without working more hours. Others see that they can't continue to work 70-80 hour weeks now that they have a child, if they are to be in the child's life. For one, the wake-up call was having a close friend, also a female executive with a young family, die of a heart-attack at a young age. Such wake-up calls raise the question: "Am I spending my energy the way I would want to if I knew that I only had X years to live?"

Use this workbook to create joy in your life.

What follows is a workbook for you to begin your blueprint for increasing joy in your life through intentionally creating your own idiosyncratic version of balance.

There are no right answers, but there are definitely *right questions.* These are provided for you. You can work on this alone, or discuss it with a friend, a colleague, or a coach.

Once you are clear about your *own* views, then you may decide to discuss it with those who would be affected by the changes in your behavior. This might include your partner, your colleagues, your subordinates and/or boss.

On the other hand, many changes can be made without any discussion. What people will notice is the Plan for Joy and Achieving Balance change in your ability to focus, your energy level, your clarity, and your ability to be 'present' in each moment. Some women report that others remark that their sense of humor is back in play.

Think-Feel-Do™ has a role in your personal plan.

Women executives, perhaps more than many other people, are models of *heart and mind*. That is, they use their brains to gather information and estimate outcomes. At the same time, they use their intuition, they pay attention to their 'feelings' and augment the facts with their sense of what is really true, what will really work. Based on the integration of those factors, they make their decision and *take action*.

We ask you to pay attention to these three dimensions: *thinking, feeling, and doing*, as you use this workbook to mold your future joyful balance.

Take your time filling out the questions below. While there are no right or wrong answers, your plan will be more successful if you take the time to answer the questions thoughtfully and honestly.

Your answers will move you through to a greater clarity about how you can create a joyful balance in your own circumstances. With creativity, with commitment, and by accepting insights and help from others, you can come closer to your ideal balance.

Begin Creating Your Personalized Plan for Achieving Balance and Experiencing Joy

Take An Inventory

What do I think *balance* would look like for me right now? *(Answer this whether or not you think it can be achieved.)*

What are the indicators that sometimes I do *not* have balance at present? *(Be specific; use examples)*

What's working now (*creates balance and joy*) and what's not working (*erodes balance and joy*)?

How is lack of balance impacting my *joy*? *(This could include health, quality of time, performance, feelings of being prepared or unprepared, scattered focus, etc.)*

Inventory Analysis Summary:

Identify Your Reference Points

Have I ever lived a balanced life? (Yes/No)

If yes, when, under what circumstances?

How are my current circumstances different from when I led a balanced life? What has changed?

Are there any clues in my changed life circumstances as to where I need to make adjustments?

Reference Point Analysis Summary:

Examine Your Roles

Let's start with an examination of your role at work.

Understanding where there is flexibility within your job will enhance your ability to create work/life balance. Achieving balance and increasing joy may require shifting your priorities and aligning your use of energy to better match your priorities.

One of the things I've observed is that executives often fail to use the available breadth of their freedom to redefine their roles. They often act as if they must (1) fulfill the role of the person who was previously in the job; or (2) carryout their role essentially as they carried out their previous role; or (3) exercise the role to the letter of the position description. *None of these is required, nor does it provide* the best guidance as to how to succeed.

Use your freedom and personal authority to redefine your role at work.

What is needed for you to succeed and for the organization to succeed is for you to determine (1) what the role *requires of anyone*; (2) what special requirements the role has at this particular time and with the specific circumstances at hand; and (3) what special gifts you bring to the role. Once you are clear as to the requirements and your capabilities and shortfalls, I recommend that you view fulfilling the various requirements of the role as a staffing puzzle.

You should personally do those aspects of the role that you (1) are qualified to do or able to learn to do; (2) are interested in doing; and (3) have the time to do. All other aspects of the role should be *arranged to be done*. This might be by judiciously delegating some work to your subordinates, your colleagues, your boss, your clients, or by other means.

That is to say, you can substantially redefine your role. *It is done all the time.* Take advantage of the precedent set by many others. It makes good sense to use your particular talents to the fullest and to transfer to others the requirements for which you are not as well equipped.

There may be situations in which you *must* take on roles for which you are not well equipped. For example, I coached a woman executive whose natural talent is strategy. She is valued highly by her Fortune 100 company. She is being tested by being placed in an Operations leadership role. The rationale is to determine her ability to survive in a situation that plays against her strength. This *is* a step in some organizations' Talent Management systems.

Nonetheless, she can surround herself with people who *are naturally* good at operations. This helps her to maintain her balance and deliver against business objectives while she learns as fast as she can.

With the exception of such test cases, most executives have far more leeway than they exercise to determine the exact nature of their roles, and the way in which they use their own individual time and energy.

An executive's responsibility is to deliver against business objectives. *How* they deliver is of far less interest to the powers that be.

Attempting to do it all yourself often works against you. This is even more the case as you move up the ladder. For instance, one coaching client was phenomenally successful at delivering business results through the field force. However, she was demanding and verbally harsh when colleagues didn't deliver. Without that toughness, she believed she couldn't get results on a timely basis. This style was a block to her upward mobility. To her credit, she experimented with a role modification. She ceased volunteering to solve every crisis presented to her and her colleagues. She stayed silent at certain points during conference calls, and she delegated some leadership roles to her subordinates.

Initially, she was quite concerned that this would result in weaker business results. To the contrary. Through her changed actions she extended her coalition of support in ways that helped deliver results more quickly. As a consequence, her candidacy for promotion was widely supported.

Given your overall function and role:

In what parts of your role do you feel you make the most important contribution?

In what parts of your role is your contribution the least differentiated (*that is, others could do the same thing*)?

What parts of your role give you the most satisfaction (*impact, learning, networking, other*)?

What parts of your role do you find burdensome in some way? *(what do you not like about them?)*

What must you *personally* do?

What can you delegate to your subordinates?

What could you delegate if you had the "right" subordinates? (*Is there a chance of re-staffing to get the "right" ones?*)

What could usefully (*and plausibly*) be transferred to other colleagues, departments, clients, vendors, etc.? (*What would it take to make this happen?*)

As an exercise, modify your current informal position description to an ideal role that you would love to have, that you could do. Place it here:

Consider whether you could migrate to this role over time. What would it take? Who would have to be influenced? Would you be more likely to successfully make this transition in roles through direct action or by using guerrilla tactics, flying under the radar?

If you were able to operate in this modified role, how would that contribute to *balance* and *joy*? Is it worth the attempt?

Work Roles Action Summary:

Now, let's examine your roles at home.

Based on the patterns I have observed among my coaching clients, adjusting to new circumstances often has a built-in lag time. That is, as their professional responsibilities increase, many women continue to carry out roles at home that require sub-optimal use of their time, given their priorities. Some women executives continue in roles at home that make no sense, even to them, once they consider the roles in light of *current* circumstances.

Use your own personal time to do those things that you most value and those things that no one else can do as you want them done.

How are you using your time outside of work? (*Chart one week's time in a journal. Try to make an entry for each 1 or 2-hour period. For each entry, mark it as joyful [+]; neutral [0]; or draining [-]. You may find some surprises.*)

What uses of time outside of work are most crucially important to you?

Which uses of time outside of work cause you to feel resentment or lack of satisfaction, perhaps that they're merely an obligation?

What activities that you perform outside of work could you:
- o Drop completely?
- o Ask someone else to do?
- o Do less often?
- o Delay and batch process (bunch together)?
- o Combine with some other activity?
- o Convert to technology-assisted ways?
- o Do with friends or family so that you would enjoy it more?
- o Do to a more relaxed standard, or in a more relaxed manner?
- o Hire someone else to do?
- o Other

What expectations of extended family and friends do you need to renegotiate?

- o Holiday roles
- o Drop-in visiting arrangements
- o Home cooking
- o Organizing presents, cards, celebrations, etc.
- o Other

What activities *would you like to do* outside of work that you never have time to do?

- o Maintenance: exercise, medical, dental, beauty, pleasure, etc.
- o Partnership: time alone with your partner, with no 'deliverables"
- o Play or quiet time with children
- o Time to be spiritually attentive
- o Play time with friends
- o Playful learning
- o Pursuing interests and hobbies
- o Whatever rejuvenates you!!
- o Other

Do you do things at home "just because"?

Some women continue to do activities that they once thought they should do, or that *others still think* they should do, without examining how they themselves truly feel about them.

For everything there is a season. You may be able to re-allocate your use of time in ways that free up time to be used for other, more important-to-you activities.

In what areas of your life do you hold standards that may be worthy of re-examination and possibly need to be changed?

- Housekeeping
- Home cooking
- Family chores (e.g., dry-cleaning, laundry)
- Gifts for kids from each trip
- Making family photo albums
- Extended-family or friends celebrations (always at your house?)
- Other?

Home Roles Action Summary:

Think about your Personal Needs

One of the first things that women sacrifice is time for themselves. Often, there is no such time left once commitments to others such as housework, profession, children, spouse, friends, and family are fulfilled. Yet, without some way of refilling the well, no woman can sustain her energy, vitality, her intellectual and spiritual health.

A touchstone that I find powerful is the image of each of us as a well. If we each imagine our energy as a well, we should always be full to overflowing. That which we give (to our families, to our friends, to our organizations) should come from the *overflow* of our excess and renewable resource, never lowering the level of resource in our own well. Let me offer financial management as a reference for our use of energy. We live a sustainable life when we live on the *interest* from our investments, as opposed to when we deplete the capital itself.

I find that renewal of energy is a crucial point of understanding for the many women executives who give and give, out of the best of intentions, the highest of professional standards, without realizing that they are literally draining themselves dry. For each such executive, there comes a day when she can give no more. That confrontation with reality takes many forms, but it cannot be avoided if we are not attending to renewing our own source. No one has more than twenty-four hours in the day, although many of us act as if we do!

What rejuvenates you?

There is no more personal and idiosyncratic question than this. For some women, revitalization comes from whitewater rafting, for others, through needlework, for others, via two unscheduled hours in which she is responsible for doing *nothing*, accountable to *no one*, and does not have to report to anyone how she has spent the time.

Find your own specific sources of renewal. I have coached people who know their own source of revitalization and who feel more guilty about engaging with that source than about any other possible use of their time. I have also worked with clients who have denied themselves for so long that they no longer *know* what would refresh them.

If you don't know what would rejuvenate you, experiment:

- o Consider things you used to do that you no longer have time to do
- o Consider activities that you enjoyed as a child
- o Consider things that you always say you *wish* you had time to do
- o Ask your women friends what they do for rejuvenation
- o Scan some books
- o Delve into what *type* of thing you are most missing:
  - physical (spa, exercise, personal trainer, dance workshop)
  - intellectual (poetry, concerts, museums,
  - books, practical skill guides);

- spiritual (weekend retreat, meditation, study groups and practice guides)

  o Do something with a friend or friends (make sure you *really* want to do it versus doing it mainly to appease friends who feel they have not had enough of your time)

Write down 2-4 potential sources of your rejuvenation.

Note: For some women it is painful to explicitly name what would bring them joy. If you notice this, be compassionate with yourself...and write it down anyway. Both conditions can exist simultaneously. You can be in pain and at the same time take actions that move you, eventually, toward something that you want deeply.

If you can't find time to do something rejuvenating right now, determine some time within the next 90 days when you can take at least 4 hours (half a day) for this purpose. Put it on the calendar. *This is the action that is most likely to be delayed or cancelled.* Anticipating that vulnerability to procrastinate, space out, to strategically forget, can help you to take special steps to ensure that you follow-through. Remember, this is for you, the person that you habitually put last. You are changing a habit when you start this piece of the change plan.

Oxygenation and Rejuvenation Action Summary:

Create your Plan for Achieving Balance and Experiencing More Joy. Really.

How to start? With a big splash, or one toe in the water?

As you consider your plan, it is worthwhile to consciously decide which change strategy will work best for you. For some women, if something is worth doing at all, it is worth doing *big*. If you are one of those, then be sure that your first step is likely to make such a significant change in how you *feel* about your work/life balance that it is worth the effort.

For others, if you have to wait until you can find the time to execute big changes, no significant change will happen soon. If this describes you, plan small, but meaningful changes. For one executive, this meant setting her alarm clock to ring one-half hour earlier and spending that time on the treadmill. It gave her a sense for the entire day that she had done *something* toward balance in her life, something that contributed to her health, raised her energy level and made a difference.

The test as to what first step is right for you is not what size of a step you can s*tart with*, but whether you can *sustain* that focus on your personal vision of work/life balance over time. Only you know what size first step is "right-sized" for sustainability.

It's time to plan your overall Plan for Achieving Balance and Experiencing More Joy.

Like other complex efforts, your *Plan for Joy* will benefit from good project planning. Project planning includes setting interim goals and measures, estimating resource requirements, scheduling calendar time, and coordinating all elements such that the project is realistic and successful. Many of my clients are so enthusiastic as they reconnect (in thought and discussion) with the sources of joy that were squeezed out of their lives, that they overestimate how much can be done. This enthusiasm is natural.

Consider your first version of the plan a draft.

Since this is a draft, you can go back and make changes. For example, a senior woman planned some long-delayed travel with her family. Once she finally coordinated everyone's calendars (her own, the children's school and social calendars, her husband's, Board meetings and other work and outside responsibilities) it took considerably longer for her to fit in all the trips that the family wanted to take. And it was worth it. Interestingly, once the full travel plan was in place, she felt fulfilled by the challenging process of involving each family member in planning for the travel, rather than frustrated by the extended timeline. The revised schedule allowed for balance in each family member's life, including hers.

Create and Adjust.

Enter into this Joy Planning as an exercise in creating and adjusting. It is a critical process that women executives perform naturally each day: prioritize; take action; re-prioritize The difference is that for your plan you will be (1) planning farther out (3-6 months); (2) giving priority to those aspects of your life that have been under-represented in ordinary on-the-run decision-making. We respond to the squeaky wheel. This planning gives you a chance to counterbalance those squeaks (conference calls, computer-scheduled meetings, budget submissions) with your own replies to the silent inner calls that must be answered in order for you to sustain your viability and energy.

Overall Plan

What are your Balance and Joy goals? What do you want to *feel* like once you have implemented this plan? What would be the indicators that you have achieved your Balance and Joy goal? *(Imagine that you have achieved these goals. As if you were in a cinema, run the movie in fast-forward and imagine yourself already having achieved these goals. What does it feel like? Notice. Breathe it in. You may want to keep that picture, that feeling as atouchstone as you create it as a reality in your life.)*

Rhonda Harper

What are the 3-5 most important changes that you want to make? These may be Start Doing, Stop Doing, and/or Do Differently.

- Review your summary notes from the above workbook sections.
- Scan any checkmarks and notes that you made in the boxes after the women's stories.
- Consider the thoughts that have been uppermost in your mind about your own life since you started this book.)

For each of those changes, what are the major Action Steps involved?

Is there a logical sequence that suggests that you should start with one particular change? (*For example, a woman might decide that she needs to say "no" to Task Force and Committee work requests in order to free up her time to do some of the other steps.*)

170 *Get to What's Real. Figure Out the Truth. Plan Joy. Experience Joy.*

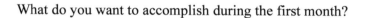

First Month

What do you want to accomplish during the first month?

What actions are you willing to commit to during the following month?

When, in the next month, can you start to carry out the planned actions suggested above? (*This is where you may learn that the actions you planned for one month will take more time. Adjust your plan, if necessary. To make it as realistic as possible, take into account (1) business imperatives such as month-end closings, year-end sales push, annual audits, budgets, and other corporate processes, etc.; (2) personal or school calendars such as holidays, parents' weekend, partner's travel. Put key actions on your calendar.*)

Schedule a Review and Celebration date with yourself 30 days from whatever date you set as your start date. *(Celebrate whatever you accomplished! This step of Stop! Look! Celebrate! is the very step that re-fuels you for the next chapter. Be compassionate about* Plan for Joy *and* Achieving Balance *whatever you did not complete. Be analytical about what you learned. Adjust. Create your plan for the next month.)*

First Quarter

What do you want to accomplish during the next Quarter?

- What specific actions will that take?
- When can you do them?

(Put key items on your calendar. Include a date in each month to check in with yourself as to how you feel, what you are doing, what you are thinking.)

Sample Actions for Achieving Balance and Experiencing More Joy

- Celebrate what *is* working; consider cloning it
- Take time alone (meal out?) with each child, with spouse
- Hire (more) help at home
- Cook on weekends for the rest of the week
- Involve children/ spouse more in household responsibilities
- Order take-out
- Live more simply (fewer frills)
- Be less of a perfectionist about housekeeping standards
- Expect adolescents to be more responsible for own laundry
- Use delivery services: dry-cleaners, gifts, groceries
- Use standard menus w/ associated shopping lists
- Take 30 minutes alone and "off-duty" (soaking bath, yoga, exercise, read)
- Walk as you talk (with family, with friends)

- Do chores with friends and/or family
- Talk to friends about their ways of creating joy and time for joy
- Re-examine the family's use of 'leisure' time: weekends, school and family vacations
- Evaluate your transition from work to personal and vice versa. Re-engineer if necessary.
- Reserve one night a week for unscheduled time
- Evaluate your use of weekend time. Redesign if warranted.
- Standardize what you can: checklists for grocery and sundries shopping; weekly schedule for meals, laundry, cleaning, school preparation, etc.
- Get more beneficial rest/sleep
- Use technology to save you time/effort
- Ask for feedback and brainstorming ideas from those who have your best interests at heart

Summary of Joy Plan for Balance:

Goal

Action Steps & Timing:

Now that you have a Joy Plan for Balance....take action!

You may feel *complete*, a sense of accomplishment. That is great! In fact, life streams so continuously for executive women that *declaring completion* may be the only way to experience it!

On the other hand, once the plan is on paper, some women feel pressured. It becomes *one more thing to do* on the endless To Do List. Take the first step. That is the action that works best in either situation. Start working your plan.

When your change actions unfurl according to plan, you may begin to feel the joy right away. Or (perfectionists take note), you may feel that it is too little, too late. Based on what has lead to success for my clients, I would encourage you to intentionally celebrate small successes. By doing so, you will find more energy to take the subsequent steps.

But what happens when your plan doesn't work? Perhaps you fail to take an action by the planned date. Or you take the action, but it doesn't have the intended effect. Especially during the early stages of such a plan, you may be demoralized, decide that the entire plan is a futile, that it is impossible to have more Joy and Balance in your life.

Let me suggest an alternative. Consider the scientific approach. Imagine yourself in a white lab coat, dispassionately examining data. In science, all data, whether indicating 'success' or 'failure', is considered valuable. A 'failure' simply tells us something did *not* work. That redirects our attention. If we can figure out *why* it did not work, all the better. Perhaps you were unrealistic in thinking that you could actually get up that one-half hour earlier every day. Perhaps you forgot that Thursday nights your mother's caretaker calls from the West Coast to bring you up to date. As a result, Thursday night can't be your *unscheduled* night.

Understanding why it didn't work may help you identify minor adjustments in order to make something similar work. But even if you have no clue as to why it didn't work, science gives you a clear directive: *Try something else.* Don't waste energy calling yourself undisciplined, unrealistic, or any other label. Try something else that gives you a chance of achieving the same goal......and move on.

Expectations and reality....managing momentum

Many people are 'high' at the beginning of this kind of project. They are reconnected to what matters in their lives, and committed to taking action toward it. Especially for the many women executives who are Type A, beginning the action promotes a feeling of well-being, taking charge.

Equally commonly, people become discouraged when the results of the change action do not fall into place quickly. For this reason, I encourage measuring success of the change plan by the month, not by the week or the day. That is, you are looking for *trends toward Balance and Joy,* not expecting instant and total success.

Reviewing how things are going, compared to plan, more frequently than monthly can be useful for the process of creating and adjusting. But don't evaluate overall success of your Plan for Achieving Balance and Experiencing More Joy every day or you may become discouraged in the early stages.

With a little help from your friends…

There is no need to do this alone, although you may prefer to do so. There is nothing wrong with that choice. However, if you decide to involve others, here are some roles that you might want to consider. Be guided by what has worked for you in the past.

- **Board of Directors for Balance**
  - o Reviews your goals, your plans, your actions against plan and serves as an advisory board to help you talk through what is working, what is not and how best to move forward.
- **Joy Team**
  - o Engages in joyful activities together with you, creates joy in their own lives (thereby spreading the joy) and in the lives of others.
- **Problem-solving Team**
  - o Individuals you can call upon when everything is falling apart…to vent your feelings safely, to get ideas as to how to get out of it or engage in damage control.

Step 4:
Experience Joy

Experience Joy

Energy is equal to desire and purpose.
- Sheryl Adams

Now that you have your *Plan for Joy and Balance*, track of your progress and allow for adjustments. The remainder of this book provides you with journaling pages to help you keep track of *what you are thinking, how you are feeling, and what you are doing.*

My *Plan for Joy* Journal:

I am no longer what I was. I will remain what I have become. – Coco Chanel

One of the quickest ways to become exhausted is by suppressing your feelings. – Sue Patton Thoele

Life is to be lived. – Katharine Hepburn

Truth has rough flavors if we bite it through.
–George Eliot

Your goal should be out of reach but not out of sight.
-Anita Defrantz

Perfectionism is self-abuse of the highest order.
- Anne Wilson Schaef

It takes a lot of courage to show your dreams to someone else. – Erma Bombeck

We don't know who we are until we see what we can do.

- Martha Grimes

Rhonda Harper

Conclusion

When you come right down to it,
the secret of having it all is loving it all.
- Dr. Joyce Brothers

On October 21, 2003 the idea of this book grabbed me and wouldn't let go for the eight days it took to to get it to the publisher on October 30. I've missed meals with my family and haven't had makeup on in days. I'm so sleep deprived I can hardly stay awake.

But I wouldn't trade these past eight days for anything.

My hope is that after reading this book you have walked away with three new, relevant ideas that can help you find *joy* and *balance* – however you choose to define it for yourself.

I have learned these three new, relevant ideas regarding the work/life balance issue:

1. ***No one has it figured out.*** Generally, women believe that they are alone in their struggle although every woman I spoke with confirmed their struggle with the balance issue.

2. ***Women are there for each other.*** Women believe that they need to deal with it alone although every woman I spoke with reinforced her commitment to helping their colleagues through their balance issues.

3. ***It is a very personal issue.*** There is no "one size fits all" way of dealing with the balance issue. Each woman I interviewed had a unique definition of balance and methods of dealing with it.

Wishing you joy.

On behalf of the Executive Corporate Women who spoke out in this book and the *Real Truth Marketing & Joy* family,

I wish you joy, - Rhonda

About the Author – Rhonda Harper

Rhonda Harper is the Founder & CEO of RTM&J, Real Truth Marketing & Joy®, a strategic brand marketing consultancy with Fortune 500 clients across many industries: consumer package goods, retail, healthcare, apparel, management consulting, communications, and entertainment.

Previously, Rhonda was responsible for some of the biggest and best brands on the planet. After stints at Nabisco, Warner-Lambert (now Pfizer) and American Red Cross, her career culminated in positions as an Officer and Vice President of Marketing for Wal-Mart Stores Inc. as well as for VF Corporation (the world's largest apparel company). In both positions Rhonda led and had direct reporting accountability for brand marketing, advertising, promotion, creative services, business insights / research, in-store merchandising, trade marketing, database management, and strategic planning.

Over the years, Rhonda also served as an evening Adjunct MBA Marketing Professor at American University and Fairleigh Dickinson. She has also been a Board Member of the Promotion Marketing Association (PMA) and Leadership Worth Following, a talent identification, assessment, and development firm.

Rhonda holds an MBA from the Goizueta Business School at Emory University and a BS from Illinois State University. She resides in Atlanta, GA, with Jim, her husband, Jayne, their daughter, and two labs Kramer and Elaine.

About Karen Searles Brethower, Ph.D.

Karen Searles Brethower, Ph.D. is the Founder and CEO of Executive Consultation LLC. Since 1989, Executive Consultation has provided Executive Coaching, Talent Selection, and Meeting Design & Facilitation to companies big and small. Her clients include Verizon, Pfizer, US Trust, Con Edison, Federal Express, Met Life and more.

In addition to ECL services, Karen has taught numerous executive development programs and serves as an international keynote speaker.

Karen is the former Vice President of Talent Management, Chase Manhattan Bank where she created their first Succession Planning System. During her period with Ford Motor Company, she spearheaded vanguard large-scale change projects. As a university professor, she taught at the University of Michigan Business School's New School for Social Research.

Karen is active within her industry as well. She has held offices in the ASTD and ISPI. Additionally, Karen served as Trustee for the Cambridge Center for Behavioral Studies. She also testified before the Senate Committee on Labor and Human Resources.

The YWCA awarded Dr. Brethower as the International Businesswoman of the Year.

DISCARD

Made in the USA